Tablets of the Heart

Order this book online at www.trafford.com/07-1850
or email orders@trafford.com

Most Trafford titles are also available at major online book retailers.

Note for Librarians: A cataloguing record for this book is available from Library and Archives Canada at www.collectionscanada.ca/amicus/index-e.html

ISBN: 978-1-4251-4401-2

 www.trafford.com

North America & international
toll-free: 1 888 232 4444 (USA & Canada)
phone: 250 383 6864 ♦ fax: 250 383 6804 ♦ email: info@trafford.com

The United Kingdom & Europe
phone: +44 (0)1865 722 113 ♦ local rate: 0845 230 9601
facsimile: +44 (0)1865 722 868 ♦ email: info.uk@trafford.com

10 9

Tablets of the Heart

Stories of Faith And Forgiveness

Jane Westmoreland

Trafford
PUBLISHING

*You yourselves
are our letter of recommendation,
written on your hearts,
to be known and read by all men;
and you show that you are
a letter from Christ delivered by us,
written not with ink
but with the Spirit of the living God,
not on tablets of stone
but on tablets of human hearts.*

2 CORINTHIANS 3:2–3

*But this is the covenant
which I will make with the house of Israel
after those days, says the Lord:
I will put my law within them,
and I will write it upon their hearts;
and I will be their God,
and they shall be my people.*

JEREMIAH 31:33

*Let not loyalty and faithfulness forsake you;
bind them about your neck,
write them on the tablet of your heart.*

PROVERBS 3:3

*My son, keep my words
and treasure up my commandments with you;
keep my commandments and live,
keep my teachings as the apple of your eye;
bind them on your fingers,
write them on the tablet of your heart.*

PROVERBS 7:1–3

---

*This book was written in memory of my parents,
the late James Horace Westmoreland
and Oletta Patterson Westmoreland.*

*It is dedicated to the Christian friends
who have celebrated the good times with me,
while sustaining me through the crises.
You know who you are.*

Acknowledgments

With heartfelt appreciation:

† *to the Esther Sunday School Class for their daily love and support which provided me with renewed inspiration to write.*

† *to Sue and Howell who are like family.*

† *to Elaine, Suzanne, Dewey, and Carol for continually blessing my life over the decades.*

† *to Angie, Paula, and Barrie for their friendship since college and their assistance with proofreading.*

† *to Dr. Sherouse for reviewing the content of this book for biblical accuracy and for making stylistic recommendations.*

Table of Contents

Introduction

In olden days salt was used to preserve foods, and a large part of each day was used planning for meals. People knew what it was like to go hungry and gave thanks to God for their food with both humility and praise. Reading or listening to the Bible was not just a spiritual choice. It was a guide for physical survival as well. We hardly think about that today as we go through the drive-through windows of fast food restaurants, purchase ready-made meals at the grocery store, or fill up on junk food at the gas station. Food is everywhere and is full of artificial preservatives that remove the fear of spoilage. Yet we are hungry. In this busy world we hunger for emotional self-preservation and turn to varying sources for relief and comfort. Some of those sources are healthy, and some are not.

Food in olden days would have perished and become useless without salt. Likewise, we as Christians become useless to the kingdom if we lose our spiritual seasoning. That seasoning comes through faith and forgiveness. Only through faith can we believe that both we and others can improve, find peace, and live joyfully. Only through forgiveness can we love both ourselves and others.

13

As we seek a life of growing faith and the power of forgiveness that brings healing, there is a light that naturally glows within us and is perceived by those who are stumbling in the darkness as a glimmer of hope. How selfish it would be for us to hide the light that would bring someone home to safety! How selfish it would be to keep the seasoning to ourselves that would enhance the spiritual growth of another child of God! We are called to do good works for the world. We are instructed that actions do not have to be hidden to be worthy. However, we are cautioned that God is to receive the glory for all that we accomplish, not ourselves.

It has taken a year and a half to write this book but a lifetime to live it. Each story was written following daily scripture readings, devotionals, and prayer. Before writing each day I asked for God's guidance in choosing words that would glorify His kingdom and further the work of His church. May these lessons of faith and forgiveness add insight and inspiration to your own spiritual journey. May God's blessings pour down upon you as you do the work necessary to allow your personal light to grow from a flicker to a beacon and to give you the motivation to share your seasoning with others. May the layers of any discomfort in your life be unfolded as you read this book so that you can find the salt and light underneath that will allow you to tolerate the intolerable and reach the unreachable. May any enlightenment that you receive from the reading of the scriptures following each story be attributed to God's loving touch on the tablets of your heart.

You are the salt of the earth;
but if salt
has lost its taste,
how shall its saltiness be restored?

It is no longer good for anything
except to be thrown out
and trodden under foot by men.

You are the light of the world.

A city set on a hill cannot be hid.

Nor do men light a lamp
and put it under a bushel,
but on a stand,
and it gives light to all in the house.

Let your light
so shine before men,
that they may see your good works
and give glory
to your Father who is in heaven.

MATTHEW 5:13–16

ONE

The Kidnapping

Griffin was a sleepy town in Georgia, known to many in the 1960's only by its proximity to Atlanta. Who would have guessed that a teenager at Griffin High School would have her parents robbed and kidnapped at gunpoint? It was ten o'clock on a Monday night before Christmas. I was at home asleep, my brother was away at college, and my parents had just closed the family business. Westmoreland's Self-Service Grocery Store was a larger than usual convenience store with a country flair. People came from all around for its specialty meats—everything from souse meat to caviar. The locals favored the homemade barbeque sauce, pimiento cheese, brunswick stew, chicken salad, and more. They also came in for conversation. The store was located in a relatively isolated spot on West McIntosh Road. Today there is a major shopping center in the location where the lonely grocery store had once stood and a Super Wal-Mart across the road, but back then there were only fields, a few scattered homes, and a couple of gas stations that had already closed for the night. There was no one to witness what was about to happen.

It was customary for my mom to go directly to the passenger side of the car when the store closed. My dad would lock the front door of the store and then proceed to the car with the cash in one hand and his pistol in the other, looking around for possible trouble. He had always been untrusting and cautious, but even his eye for detail could not protect them that night from what the Georgia Bureau of Investigation later described as a professional criminal. An intruder unexpectedly appeared from around the corner of the building. In an instant he grabbed my dad, who attempted to point the pistol at his assailant. There was a brief struggle, and the gun went off. No one was hit. The stranger used a martial arts maneuver that allowed him to confine my dad and confiscate his pistol. The cash bag was surrendered without further resistance in hopes that the thief would declare himself the victor and leave. However, he had other plans. Pressing the gun against my dad's back, he instructed him to get behind the wheel. The thief climbed into the back seat where he pulled out a pistol of his own. Now pointing one firearm at the back of each of my parents' heads, he commanded my dad to exit right out of the parking lot.

It was a dark, rainy night. There was little traffic, and visibility was low. As they moved 40 miles an hour down the two-lane road in the direction of Fayetteville, the intruder mumbled complacently, "I ought to hurt you for what you tried back there with your pistol." My mom stared straight ahead and made no sound, knowing it best to let my dad handle the situation without interference. Again, the intruder insisted, "I ought to hurt you for what you tried back there with your pistol." My dad's perception, through listening to their abductor as he drove, was that he would be shot in the back of the head when they reached their destination and that my mother would be soiled and left for dead. He had already failed once in handling the situation and knew he would have only one more opportunity.

Glaring at a well-known house on the right side of the road, with what appeared that night as an unusually long and curved driveway, he whipped the car at a right angle into the sheriff's driveway without any decrease in speed so that the stranger would be unsuspecting. My dad fully anticipated that the gun pointed at the back of his head would be fired at that point but that my mother might have a chance to escape. Because of the weather, the speed of the car, and the curvature of the driveway the car began to spin out of control and hit a large tree head-on. During those days seatbelts were neither fashionable nor required, and air bags did not exist. Just before impact my dad threw out his right arm in an attempt to keep my mom's petite body in place. However, the crash was overpowering. His head was thrust into the windshield, while the steering wheel braced the forward movement of his body. My mom's head was protected from going through the windshield by my dad's arm, but her knees sank into the glove compartment. The thief opened the back door and ran carrying both pistols and the sack of money with him. Not realizing the tendon in her right leg had been completely severed or that her left foot was broken, my mom attempted to step out of the car to see which way he had gone. She collapsed in the mud.

By then my dad was pounding on the door of the sheriff's house with a bloodied face yelling for help, dogs barking and running wildly in the yard. The sheriff's wife, who was at home alone with her daughter, put in phone calls for immediate assistance and knew not to open the door until they arrived. Within seconds sheriff's deputies surrounded the area. Griffin was a small town where everybody knew everybody, and if you didn't you were supposed to. All were so attentive to my parents' needs that they failed to notice a car speeding down West McIntosh Road headed east–a car, it was later determined, that was most likely the thief's get-away vehicle, perhaps with an accomplice driving. An ambulance rushed my parents to the hospital.

One of the deputies brought the sheriff's daughter, who was a friend of mine from high school, with him over to our house so that I would know that it was safe to answer the door. We lived in the country, and I had also been taught not to open the door without knowing who was on the other side. Before I could speak to them the phone rang. It was my aunt telling me that she and my uncle were on the way over. They lived in a house between the store and the sheriff's house, had heard on the radio what had happened, and wanted to break the news to me in person, not on the phone. Still drowsy from being awakened on a school night, and trying to mentally process why there were so many visitors that time of night, I responded, "Mama and Daddy are not home yet, but you know you are always welcome."

The deputy did not want to alarm me with how badly my mother had been hurt, so he attempted to downplay her injuries and to focus on my dad's condition which I misconstrued in an air of panic. All I remembered hearing was the deputy saying, "There's been a robbery by a man with a gun. Your mom is going to be fine. Your dad got hit in the head." What? There was a gun? My mom was fine, but my dad got hit in the head? I thought he meant my dad had been shot in the head! I thought my dad might be dead! The deputy and the sheriff's daughter waited patiently at the door while I tried to comprehend the events of the evening.

In less than two minutes my aunt and uncle were there ready to take me to the hospital where my parents were in the emergency room. The phone rang once more. It was the hospital. My mother's thoughts had turned from the robbery, the kidnapping, and the wreck to her teenage daughter hearing the news at home alone. The doctor had explained the seriousness of her injuries, and she insisted on talking to me before they gave her anesthesia to let me know everything would be fine. After hearing from her I asked to speak to my dad. Over and over I asked if my dad was all right, but she was fading from the medication and gave no response. A nurse had lifted the phone from my mother's hand to roll her into surgery and told me they would take good care of her. Was my dad dead? There was no conversation on the way to the hospital, but I remember asking God over and over again for help.

It would be an understatement to say that I was relieved, upon arriving at the hospital, to hear that my dad was alive. The relief was replaced, however, by the horror of my mother's condition. I was asked to sit in the waiting room while my aunt and uncle went to talk to the doctor. They were told my dad had stitches in his forehead and was shaken up, but he would be fine and could take me back home. It was late by then, my aunt and uncle were elderly, and my dad suggested they go back home after thanking them for their help. He assured them I would be fine in the waiting room until he could get there.

It seemed like an eternity sitting in the waiting room by myself. I'll never forget a policeman who was so gentlemanly in not encroaching upon my space but tried to let me know he was there for me if I needed anything. As I sat in the quietness of the dimly lit room in those early morning hours, my mind shifted to all the Sunday School lessons of a lifetime. I prayed silently, and a peace came over me. It was a time for leaning on God's comfort and mercy in the midst of the fear, helplessness, and hopelessness. Surgery took several hours. Yet, I knew I was not alone and that I would never be alone.

My dad remained close to the operating room until the surgery was over. Then he came to sit with me. I had never seen him so shaken up. His clothes were bloodied, and his forehead was full of stitches. He was hoarse from yelling so loudly for help in the sheriff's yard and from explaining everything in such detail to the authorities and the media. He was weak, and I knew it was not the time for us to talk. The tendon in my mom's right leg required over 300 stitches. Her left knee had been damaged and required surgery as well, and there was the broken foot. My parents were alive, though, and how I thanked God for that!

I learned that night what it truly meant to have faith, not

just to speak of it. It was in the days ahead, though, that I was to learn what it was to forgive as I observed the physical trials and the emotional aftermath of the trespasser's violation of my family.

Two sheriff's deputies escorted my dad and me home from the hospital once my mom was out of surgery and out of danger. They walked through the house to make sure there was no one inside, telling us that aggravated thieves had been known to return and retaliate against those who had not given in to them willingly. I'll never forget my dad showing me how to use a rifle that night before we retired, and he slept with one in the bed by his side until my mom came home, at which time a new pistol was positioned on his night stand for easy access.

The local authorities and the Georgia Bureau of Investigation worked diligently on the case, but no arrests were made. For months my dad was looking over his shoulder everywhere he went, as though someone was standing ready to overpower him or to hurt a loved one, and wanting to make sure he was more prepared this time. My mom couldn't walk independently for several months but only limped slightly into her senior years. She was so grateful to all who visited her, who sent cards, and who phoned her. She told everyone how hard my dad had tried that night to keep them both safe and how I was doing all of the housework, finishing the Christmas shopping, preparing meals, and running errands. I don't recall her ever complaining about the pain but will always remember how strange it was to see such a previously vibrant and energetic woman moving about so slowly and having to depend on a walker to get from room to room.

My love and appreciation of my parents deepened through that ordeal, and I related to them differently from that point forward. My love and appreciation of God also deepened through that experience. It was only through His grace and His mercy that my parents were still alive and able to function normally. I knew that when the day came that I no longer had my parents with me, I would not be alone but would be sustained by His love. I knew that whatever life was to offer me in the future that I could depend on God to get me through it. It was not until decades later that I learned how much I would really need that faith or that I pondered the strength it took for my parents to forgive their trespasser. It was not until decades later that I understood that forgiveness is not merely something we do for someone else; it is something we do for ourselves in order to move forward.

So faith comes from what is heard,
and what is heard
comes by the preaching of Christ.

ROMANS 10:17

Let all bitterness and wrath
and anger and clamor and slander
be put away from you,
with all malice,
and be kind to one another,
tenderhearted, forgiving one another,
as God in Christ forgave you.

EPHESIANS 4:31–32

And forgive us our debts,
As we also have forgiven our debtors.

MATTHEW 6:12

For if you forgive men their trespasses,
your heavenly Father also
will forgive you;
but if you do not forgive men their trespasses,
neither will your Father forgive
your trespasses.

MATTHEW 6:14–15

The Lord is a stronghold for the oppressed,
a stronghold in times of trouble.
And those who know thy name put their trust in thee,
for thou, O Lord,
hast not forsaken those who seek thee.

PSALM 9:9–10

Prayer

Heavenly Father, we praise You for being our stronghold in times of trouble and for Your promises which go unchanged. We know that You will not forsake us if we put our trust in You. Open our hearts to those who have offended us and wounded our spirits that we might forgive them as You have forgiven us.

Please help us as adults to comprehend how important it is to get children to church where they can learn the biblical principles that will sustain them through life. Keep the children protected through Your power and through their growing faith. Teach them the healing that comes from forgiveness.

TWO

Who is Really in Control Here?

It was 2:00 A.M. when the phone call came telling me that my dad, who was in his seventies and had terminal lung cancer, had been rushed to the hospital. I was an elementary school teacher in my mid-forties, asleep with a husband by my side, when the call came. My dad's other health problems, combined with his age, had ruled out surgery or chemotherapy as an option for treating the cancer. Radiation treatments had begun just before Thanksgiving, each treatment leaving him weaker than before. It had not been unusual during the previous months for him to be rushed to the hospital for one reason or another, but this time my mother's voice sounded more frantic than usual. I did not hear fear in her voice as much as a sense of failure or a sense of guilt, which was something new. After an hour's drive to the hospital in Griffin, I entered the door of the Intensive Care Unit and immediately understood the urgency of her tone. The medics had hooked my dad up to life support.

How could this have happened? He had a Living Will preventing such. My mother had carried a copy in her purse for months for emergency purposes. My dad had kept a copy by the hospital bed that had been moved into their home weeks

earlier, and it was transported on his chest in the ambulance
each time he went to the hospital. The doctor had been told
repeatedly by my dad that under no circumstances was he ever
to be placed on life support. I looked at him, tubes forced
inside of him and taped to his face, with a machine next to
the bed that was breathing for him. "What is this machine?" I
asked the nurse, seeking confirmation of what was apparent.
"Why has he been placed on it?" No one at the hospital seemed
to know that he was not supposed to be on life support, and
they could not take him off without his doctor present. They
explained that sometimes it happened. People would become
frantic in an emergency and forget to mention the Living Will
or to produce it. Time is of the essence in saving a life, and no
one takes the time to check the records or put in a call to the
doctor because a life could be lost in the process.

It was then that I knew my dad had been unable to grasp
his paperwork when the ambulance arrived to pick him up,
and my mom was either too rattled or emotionally unable to
give the hospital the copy in her purse. It was inconsequential
at that moment why it happened or who was at fault. All that
mattered was that my dad – a man who had insisted, begged,
and demanded during his latter years not to be put on life
support – was now being sustained by a machine. My heart
sank. I sent my mom home to rest. Her hands were shaking,
and her tiny body had already been reduced to 90 pounds
from the stress of his illness.

All night I sat in a chair in the corner of the room awaiting the moment when he would awaken to find himself part
machine, part man – the worst nightmare of his senior years.
For hours I pondered what I would say to him, knowing all
those times we promised him this would not happen. Then
his body began to move slightly, and his eyes opened drows-
ily. I'll never forget the look of devastation on his face as he
turned his head to the right and saw the mechanical beast.
He shook his head back and forth to communicate, "No!" in

insistence and desperation. He lifted his right hand and began feeling the hoses that constrained him, then looked at me with a pain that pierced my being. Again, he turned his head to the right looking at the machine, then pointed to it with his left hand, and looked back at me awaiting the grim confirmation of that which he already knew to be true.

My dad was not one to be fooled, and he had raised me to treasure honesty. I held his hand, looked him straight in the eye, and said in my most loving, authoritative school teacher voice, "There was a mistake, and you were put on a respirator, but they are going to take you off of it as soon as the doctor arrives. I promise your wishes will be respected. Try to rest. The doctor will be here first thing in the morning." A burden appeared to be lifted from his shoulders, and he drifted back to sleep. He awakened two more times during the night and pointed at the machine while looking to me for answers and reassurance. Two more times I told him with great command that the doctor would be there at 8:00 o'clock in the morning, and the machine would be removed. With each assurance he became relieved and fell back to sleep. He knew, with the angered conviction of the third assurance, that he did not have to fight that battle – that I would do it for him. I knew that loving my dad meant letting him go, but it was a battle that would have to wait. I closed my eyes and prayed. A glimmer of faith filled the cavity of helplessness, and I was reminded once again of the strength available through God when challenged with an "I can't fix it" situation.

A few hours can seem like weeks when you know a loved one has a need, but at last the doctor arrived. My dad was awake, and I said to him with the doctor standing there, "Your doctor is here. He knows you have a Living Will. He knows how many times you have told him that you do not want to be on life support. He is going to unhook the machine." My dad nodded to the affirmative. The doctor nodded back to him in the affirmative. Then the doctor took me into the hall and broke the news that my dad would survive less than three hours once the machine was unhooked. There was nothing that pained me more than the thought of losing him, but I knew that decision had been made with guidance from above. It was not about me. It was about him. It was about the choice of living with dignity or not living at all. It was about accepting death without man-made interference. It was about that which was legal and enforceable.

As I pondered the three hours that my dad would have left, the doctor gave a young nurse the order to unhook the machine. She refused. There was continued resistance. He left her no choice. She obeyed the doctor's instructions and removed the life-sustaining machinery from my dad. Her face was flushed, she appeared frightened, and her eyes were filled with tears. It was apparent that she was betraying her own beliefs, but I could not focus on her needs at that moment. Only later did I realize the struggle within the nurse about such life and death situations. I realized it exactly six hours after the respirator was unplugged, as she went about her job joyfully, and as my dad sat up in bed fully alert and energetic wanting to know why no one had brought him any breakfast or lunch! He did not die within three hours, or even that day or week or month.

It was then that I was reminded who was really in control. It wasn't the doctor who gave the order to remove the respirator, the nurse who followed it, the legal system that allowed it, or the family that found the love to respect it. God was not ready for my dad to come home. It was not yet his time. I believe it was God's way of looking down at us and saying, "You folks down there just THINK you are in charge." It was on that day that the Sovereign of the universe prevented circumstances from coming to pass. We learned a lesson that day that added value to our lives as a result of God's mercy. My dad lived another six months and died peacefully at home in his sleep.

For everything there is a season,
and a time for every matter under heaven:

a time to be born, and a time to die;

a time to plant,
and a time to pluck up what is planted;

a time to kill, and a time to heal;

a time to break down, and a time to build up;

a time to weep, and a time to laugh;

a time to mourn, and a time to dance;

a time to cast away stones,
and a time to gather stones together;

a time to embrace,
and a time to refrain from embracing;

a time to seek, and a time to lose;

a time to keep, and a time to cast away;

a time to rend, and a time to sew;

a time to keep silence, and a time to speak;

a time to love, and a time to hate;

a time for war, and a time for peace.

What gain has the worker from his toil?

ECCLESIASTES 3:1–9

Prayer

Heavenly Father, we praise You for the gift of life. We acknowledge that death is a natural occurrence and that only You are in control of those circumstances that we seek so passionately to manipulate. Thank You for letting us lean on You in our times of mourning and for the opportunity to rejoice with You as pleasant memories sustain us.

We acknowledge that the crucifixion of Jesus cleansed us of our sins, provided us with forgiveness for our unholy ways, and opened the door to the next life. Help us to grow in faith as we are blessed with Your continued grace and mercy. Help us to keep our focus on You instead of on our problems.

THREE

But Mama Died on Christmas Day

It was 10:00 o'clock on Christmas morning when Mother took her last breath. I stood next to her bed, holding her hand, in a small metro-Atlanta Hospice facility gazing down on what I knew had just become an empty 60 pound shell, void of a living spirit. My mind flashed back to the events of the previous weeks.

Lung cancer had overcome Mother at age 80. She had been diagnosed as terminal just before Thanksgiving, her then 90 pound body too frail to endure surgery or chemotherapy. Mother had received only a few radiation treatments when the sitter, who had been hired to live with her before she was diagnosed with cancer, phoned me at the elementary school in another county where I worked. My fourth graders were gleefully packing up their things to go home for winter break following the Christmas party when I was called to the phone. "You must come now," the sitter said seriously. "The doctor put your Mother back in the hospital. Her lungs are filled with fluid, and he said you need to come now." After giving the children a quick hug, and explaining the need for an early exit to my administrator, I headed for the hospital in Griffin.

On the one hour drive I reflected on the end that I knew

was near. My dad, a heavy smoker as well, had died of lung cancer a few years before. Mother had begun smoking again almost immediately after he was buried. It seemed somewhat like a death wish, being so alone without him in a void that no other human could fill. They had been married over half a century. She was brilliant but raised in a time when women did not seriously pursue a career. Family was everything. She had been the youngest in a large family and was the only one left, now without a spouse, with a son whose wife was dying of cancer and required his presence, with myself, and a handful of relatives in various cities and states. The sitter had to resign that week due to her sister's newly diagnosed terminal illness. I knew, for the most part, it would just be my mom, God, and me on this journey.

On the way to the hospital I prayed that she would have as little pain and discomfort as possible during her remaining time. The doctor had just finished draining her lungs when I arrived. He held up the huge, bulging sack of fluid, shaking his head with despair, as he exited her room. He explained that she was too weak to endure any more radiation treatments and had only a short time left. He could not predict how long, and I knew from my dad's illness that predictions were not always accurate.

It was five days before Christmas, and the next few days and nights were strenuous for both of us. She was having bouts of pain, and I was exhausted from a lack of sleep from spending both days and nights at the hospital. The relationship between my mother and me had become strained over the years, and I finally did what I should have done much earlier. Taking her hand and leaning over her bed, I looked into her eyes and said with the utmost love and sincerity, "Mother, will you forgive me for anything I've ever said or done to hurt you?" She looked at me with controlled annoyance and replied, "UH-UH." What a shock! Was she teasing? Was she trying to be humorous? This was the woman who had taught me as a child that when you are hurting, the best thing to do is find a way to give to others. This was a woman who had made sure I went to church, was baptized, and led a respectable life. This was a God-fearing woman who was denying her only daughter forgiveness on the only occasion in which it had ever been sought. What now?

The day before Christmas Eve had arrived, and my thoughts had shifted away from my needs and back to Mother's. What do you give someone for Christmas who is dying? The hospital was decorated for the occasion, the staff joyfully hummed yuletide tunes, and visitors brought homemade confections to the nurse's station for all to share. My mind traveled back in time to all those holiday seasons when Mother and I spent the week before Christmas making homemade treats for the traditional Open House in our home. There was always my grandmother's recipe for Japanese fruitcake that stole the show – one of those recipes you were instructed at a very early age to keep in the family. The best linens were draped across the dining room table and were adorned with at least forty varieties of appetizers, finger foods, and desserts all prepared by the two of us. The best dishes were used, and the food was available whenever anyone wanted to partake. My mother had painted china for a hobby, and the culinary treats were only surpassed by the aesthetics of the tableware. The spicy aroma of hot Russian Tea filled the house with competition only from cups of homemade eggnog which made their way into the kitchen pantry for a discreet "doctoring up" that no one was supposed to notice.

Putting up the Christmas tree was always a family affair, and every Christmas Eve was filled with happy anticipation of Santa's arrival. Laughter filled the house each Christmas morning as wrapping paper and ribbon hurled through the air revealing every gift that children could possibly want. At the end of Christmas Day I would always think to myself that there was no way the next Christmas could be as wonderful as that one, but my mom and dad had that special flair for putting the "WOW!" into each subsequent Christmas even more successfully than before.

Mother continued to sleep in the hospital room while I pondered what to get her for Christmas. This time my mind flashed back to my first Christmas at home as an adult. I was twenty-one years old, and the time had come to reciprocate. It was my first Christmas out of college and with a teacher's paycheck. My brother was working in Alaska and would not be home for the holidays. I was teaching high school that year in a nearby town and went home the day before Christmas Eve to be with my parents, my heart filled with the joy of giving and the anticipation of surprising them this year. On Christmas morning, when they arose, what they found was that Santa had come to visit THEM! A poem on the mantle read,

> "'Twas the night before Christmas,
> and down from the shelf,
> Jumped a tiny little figure,
> Known to most as an elf –
> Whose mission it had been
> To shop in Atlanta
> For goodies to give to
> The Mrs. and Santa!"

Below the note hung two floor-length stockings filled with presents, and below those were stacks of gifts wrapped in white meat-wrapping paper, like that used in my dad's grocery store, arranged just as they had been for two decades before, only this time for the adults.

What laughter filled the house that Christmas morning! What a surprise it was for my parents and a genuine joy for me to be on the other end of the giving at such a special time! How grand it was in my eyes when my dad did his Santa Claus laugh to signal it was time to open the gifts!

And now it was almost thirty years later. My dad had already died, my mom was in the process of dying, and I wanted to do something special for her for Christmas. The doctor walked into the hospital room as I reflected on how meaningless material gifts would be that year, and he asked permission to put a food tube in her tiny, sixty pound, failing body. I looked at her painfully, observing the ribs and hip bones protruding like some refugee survivor and glared at the doctor with horror. "You can't save her," I said to him through the tears. "That's already been done." He sighed with resignation as I announced, "I'm going to take her to Hospice."

For five days I had pondered this decision, had gathered information from the hospital, and had left my mother with a friend for two hours while visiting a nearby facility since there was not one in Griffin at that time. It was suddenly so clear that this was to be my Christmas present to my mother. She would be allowed to die with comfort and dignity. There would be no food tubes, no more blood pressure checks, no suspension devices for weighing her, no more waking her up for tests. There would be no delays for pain medication because nurses could administer it themselves at the Hospice facility. There would be a cozy room decorated like a bedroom that was quiet, warm, and peaceful where the last hours of Mother's life could be a private time with those who loved her.

We arrived at the Hospice in Riverdale on Christmas Eve morning. For years Mother had insisted on not being placed in a nursing home, and the prospect remained on her mind. She was not awake much of the time, but her first question when she opened her eyes was, "What is this place?" I replied, "I've brought you to Hospice, Mama. This is my Christmas present to you. I will not leave your side." She smiled sweetly and drifted off to sleep.

A staff member walked in with a plate of spaghetti, bread, dessert, and tea. "Oh," I said, "She is no longer able to swallow solid food." The nurse smiled and said, "This is for you. We want you to have some lunch. Then we will talk." The tears streamed down my face at such a kind gesture.

Mother's doctor had given me medication for my own respiratory problems that were getting increasingly worse from lack of sleep and nourishment, and I had been fighting a low-grade fever that was leaving me weak. I couldn't even remember when I had eaten last. It was the best food in the world! It was not just physically nourishing, though. The nurse's thoughtfulness and loving smile fed my spirit when she handed me that plate. I had never been one to ask for help or to want to impose, but I seldom forgot those who could tell when there was a need and responded to it. Afterwards, the staff briefed me on the dying process so that I would know what to expect. They made sure I knew that they were available to me on a second's notice, whether to help my mother or to minister to me. It was a peaceful atmosphere encompassed with love and compassion.

In a private moment on that Christmas Eve in the Hospice facility, I once again held my mother's hand, leaned over her bed, and said to her quietly, "Mother, will you forgive me for anything I've ever said or done that hurt you?" She responded most emphatically, "No."

About 9:00 o'clock that night, while she was sleeping, a different nurse came in with a beautiful Christmas tree ornament. It was a white snowflake that had been tatted. She said that her grandmother had always told her that a proper southern lady must know how to tat and that she had just been sitting at the desk finishing the delicate piece of lace. She handed me the snowflake and explained, "It's Christmas Eve, and I wanted you to have something beautiful." Again, the tears came. Such a special gift! Again, my spirit was fed. I slept on a cot next to my mother's bed that night. It was the first time in a week that either of us had slept through the night.

It was Christmas morning. We had been at the Hospice facility for less than twenty-four hours. A staff member had told me that the average stay there was eleven days, but I knew we would not be there that long. My mind was on the sitter.

She had been in tears a week earlier when she told me she had to resign to take care of her sister who lived in town and was dying of cancer as well. She was so afraid that I would feel she was deserting both Mother and me at such a crucial time. She could not apologize enough and said she hoped I would forgive her. Mother was sleeping, so I wrote a letter to the sitter letting her know where we were, that she was certainly forgiven (although there was nothing in my mind that she had done wrong), and that I was thankful for the opportunity of spending Mother's final days with her.

As I was writing, Mother opened her eyes as wide as they would open, and they shone brightly in a way that I would not have deemed possible. I walked to her side and took her hand just as she said, "Do you know who I just saw?" I responded, "No, Mother, who did you just see?" She said, "I just saw my husband." It was the only time she had ever referred to my dad using the words "my husband." She had always referred to him in front of me as "your father." There was such a sweet smile on her face and a complacent understanding followed by silence. Then she closed her eyes to nap while I finished the letter to the sitter.

It was no sooner finished than Mother opened her eyes again. This time they appeared to be open even wider and shone more brightly than before. That same sweet smile appeared. Again, I took her hand and said for the third time that week, "Mother, will you forgive me for anything I've ever said or done that hurt you?"

Her body had appeared motionless from the neck down since we had arrived at Hospice, and her arms were positioned next to her sides on top of the covers with palms down and fingers stretched straight out. Staring straight ahead at the wall, as though she was looking at some jubilant splendor more magnificent than words could describe, her head moved as far up as it could go and then as far down as it could go in a huge affirmative nod. It was then that she gave me the "Yes" she knew was necessary. It was not her usual nod, though. At that moment it was more as though someone was holding her head between their hands and moving it in the full range a healthy neck could accommodate, giving an almost lifeless body the ability to move one last time. As I said, "I love you, Mama," she took a very deep last breath, and her spirit left her body in what appeared to require far more energy and effort than they show in the movies but without prolonged delay.

I stood there and held her hand for a short while, but it took little insight to acknowledge that she was no longer in that room. Her body was very much just an empty shell. There was forgiveness on Christmas Day–more than just mine–forgiveness, love, compassion, understanding, humility, peace, truth, sacrifice–all that is holy. Those were the gifts that showered that room on Christmas Day. They were the gifts that truly counted and which material things will never equal or supercede. The "WOW!" had been put in Christmas one more time.

Many comments were made to me about how sad it was that my mother died on Christmas Day and how I would always hate Christmas because of it. However, I knew my mother would not have wanted that, and my dad would never have believed I would allow it to happen. Visions of Mother and Daddy reunited in another life imparted a strength that was to last throughout future years.

My mind shifted to the past again. Mother had once taught my Sunday School class, and my dad had once been a deacon at the church just down the road from the farm where we lived. My grandparents had contributed the communion table, and it was in that church that I had learned the lessons that were to sustain me through life. I would have to take those thoughts with me into each Christmas in the future.

Yes, Christmas is a difficult time, but I refuse to give in to negative feelings and yield to enemy powers in such a holy season. Instead, I try each year to put the "WOW" in somebody else's Christmas. I choose to cherish my memories of

Christmas with the two people who loved me in only the way that parents can. I choose to rejoice on their behalf that my mother got to make her transition on such a special day. I know with all of my heart that there is no gift you can buy, or food you can make, that will feed the inner spirit like holy gifts. The presents around the tree each year had been merely symbols of the true gift – the Christ child – and the completion that he represents.

Christ was born in a time of chaos, and I came to understand that it was all right in my life if Christmas included chaos. Christmas is a reminder that Christ brought the gift of hope with his birth, gave forgiveness through his blood when he died on the cross, and offered reassurance in the resurrection and ascension. It is a reminder that life never ends; it only changes.

The Birth

Now the birth of Jesus Christ took place in this way.

When his mother Mary had been betrothed to Joseph, before they came together she was found to be with child of the Holy Spirit; and her husband Joseph, being a just man and unwilling to put her to shame, resolved to divorce her quietly.

But as he considered this, behold, an angel of the Lord appeared to him in a dream, saying, "Joseph, son of David, do not fear to take Mary your wife, for that which is conceived in her is of the Holy Spirit; she will bear a son, and you shall call his name Jesus, for he will save his people from their sins."

All this took place to fulfill what the Lord had spoken by the prophet:

"Behold, a virgin shall conceive and bear a son, and his name shall be called Emmanuel" (which means, God with us).

When Joseph woke from sleep, he did as the angel of the Lord commanded him; he took his wife, but knew her not until she had borne a son; and he called his name Jesus.

MATTHEW 1:18–25

The Death

Then the soldiers of the governor took Jesus into the praetorium, and they gathered the whole battalion before him.

And they stripped him and put a scarlet robe upon him, and plaiting a crown of thorns they put it on his head, and put a reed in his right hand.

And kneeling before him they mocked him, saying, "Hail, King of the Jews!" And they spat upon him, and took the reed and struck him on the head.

And when they had mocked him, they stripped him of the robe, and put his own clothes on him, and led him away to crucify him.

MATTHEW 27:27–31

And when they came to the place which is called The Skull, there they crucified him, and the criminals, one on the right and one on the left.

And Jesus said, "Father, forgive them; for they know not what they do." And they cast lots to divide his garments.

It was now about the sixth hour, and there was darkness over the whole land until the ninth hour, while the sun's light failed; and the curtain of the temple was torn in two.

Then Jesus, crying with a loud voice, said, "Father, into thy hands I commit my spirit!" And having said this he breathed his last.

LUKE 23:33–34, 44–46

The Resurrection

*Next day, that is, after the day of Preparation, the chief priests
and the Pharisees gathered before Pilate and said, "Sir, we
remember how that impostor said while he was still alive, 'After three days I will rise again.' Therefore order the sepulcher
to be made secure until the third day, lest his disciples go and
steal him away, and tell the people, 'He has risen from the
dead,' and the last fraud will be worse than the first." Pilate
said to them, "You have a guard of soldiers; go, make it as
secure as you can." So they went and made the sepulcher
secure by sealing the stone and setting a guard.*

*Now after the Sabbath, toward the dawn of the first day of
the week, Mary Magdalene and the other Mary went to see
the sepulcher. And behold, there was a great earthquake; for
an angel of the Lord descended from heaven and came and
rolled back the stone, and sat upon it. His appearance was
like lightning, and his raiment white as snow. And for fear of
him the guards trembled and became like dead men. But the
angel said to the women, "Do not be afraid; for I know that
you seek Jesus who was crucified. He is not here; for he has
risen, as he said. Come see the place where he lay. Then go
quickly and tell his disciples that he has risen from the dead,
and behold, he is going before you to Galilee; there you will
see him. Lo, I have told you." So they departed quickly from
the tomb with fear and great joy, and ran to tell his disciples.
And behold, Jesus met them and said, "Hail!" And they came
up and took hold of his feet and worshiped him. Then Jesus
said to them, "Do not be afraid; go and tell my brethren to
go to Galilee, and there they will see me."*

MATTHEW 27:62–66 AND 28:1–10

The Ascension

Then he led them out as far as Bethany,
and lifting up his hands
he blessed them.

While he blessed them,
he parted from them,
and was carried up into heaven.

LUKE 24:50–51

Prayer

Heavenly Father, we give thanks for the birth of Jesus. Keep us reminded that he was born in a time of chaos and that it is unrealistic for us to expect every Christmas in our lives to be a time void of chaos or pain. Help us to remember that Christmas is not about materialism but about the gift of Your Son as our Savior. We ask that You would fill our hearts and minds with the holy gifts that we can share with others during the Christmas season and throughout the year—forgiveness, love, compassion, understanding, humility, peace, truth, and sacrifice. We pray that our focus would remain on that which Christmas truly represents. May our faith be strengthened, and our willingness to forgive be increased, during this holy season.

FOUR

On Prejudice: The Z.T. Story

It was my first year as an elementary school teacher. It was the beginning of a racially integrated school system in a nearby rural Georgia town where many lessons were being learned both by the children and the adults. I had not been raised to be racially prejudiced. That was because of Z.T., and I learned a valuable lesson on that first day with a class of first graders. A little white boy got angry with a little black boy and said to the African American in his meanest voice, "You're a honky." The little black boy wrinkled his brow and said back to him with condescendence, "I ain't no honky. You a honky. I'm a n_____."

It had never been so clear that prejudice is a learned response. Both children had learned at home that the world was black and white and that there were hurtful words to be used as verbal ammunition against the other. I grabbed the two six year olds up by their arms and said firmly, "Look, sweethearts, we're all just folks. It doesn't matter what color skin we have. All that matters is what is inside of us. Now, how about telling each other you are sorry for any hurtful statements, and let's go out for an early recess." Children, being more forgiving than adults, seldom hold grudges. The two boys smiled at

48 *Tablets of the Heart*

the idea of an early recess, shook hands, and played together without incident. They had no other problems getting along the rest of the year.

While supervising the children at play my mind reflected back on Z.T., the black man who had come to live on my dad's farm when I was a student in elementary school. It was the custom in Griffin for businesses to close at noon on Wednesdays, so that was when my dad would go to the unemployment office, get two or three workers, and bring them home to help with jobs on the farm. He had never complained about the quality of help he got or made mention of anyone who did a particularly fine job. He was simply thankful there were people who needed a half day's work at a reasonable wage.

One Wednesday, though, I remembered hearing him tell my mom that one of the workers he had brought home had done an astonishingly good job. His name was Z.T. He appeared to be in his teens, but Daddy said he had done the work of three men in one afternoon. He had told Z.T. he would ask for him if he was still at the unemployment office the next Wednesday, which he was. Over the next few weeks my dad watched Z.T.'s work and enjoyed both his smile and his joyful attitude. Z.T. never seemed to stop smiling and most assuredly never complained. He took pride in his work and seemed as grateful for the conversation as for the wages. One Wednesday afternoon my dad said to Z.T., "I surely wish I had somebody who works as hard as you do living on this farm and helping me out regularly."

A few days later there was a knock at the back door. It was Z.T. He looked up at my dad with his usual smile and said, "Mr. James, did you mean what you said about wanting someone like me to come live on your farm and work here?" They talked for a short time, and my dad learned that Z.T. was having great difficulty paying rent, buying food, and finding employment. He told Z.T. he didn't have anything to offer him except a little wooden building on the property but that he could live there free of charge if he would just help him out some in between other jobs. Daddy told him to have all his belongings ready the next Wednesday so that he could move him in his pick-up truck.

That next Wednesday Daddy showed up at the address given with his truck, and Z.T. came out with a bundle of clothes wrapped in a single sheet. Daddy said, "Come on. Let's go get the rest of your things."

Z.T. laughed and responded, "There ain't no more. This is everything."

With compassion my dad asked, "Do you have a bed or a mattress that you sleep on? Do you have any furniture?"

"No sir, Mr. James, I sleeps on the floor. There ain't no furniture."

Daddy didn't feel so badly, all of a sudden, moving Z.T. into the old wooden building on the property. He put a bed in there, made sure he ate well, and told him if he turned out to be as good of a worker as he thought he was, he would build him a better house.

My dad and Z.T. became more than employer and employee. They became friends. It soon became apparent that theirs was to become a permanent arrangement. My dad built Z.T. a concrete block house on a beautiful plot on the farm with a fenced-in yard that was surrounded by rolling green pastures. His view in every direction was nature, but he was within walking distance of our home. It was maybe a fourth of a mile away, just over a hill. Daddy made sure Z.T. had everything he needed in his new place – heat, fans, a stove, a refrigerator, a well, and all the food he needed. He taught Z.T. how to drive the tractor and to cut the pastures. He taught him how to string barbed wire. He taught him how to herd cattle and how to grow a garden. Their friendship continued to grow. Each needed the other's help. Each appreciated the other's willingness to be there in time of need.

It was still the South, however, and racial prejudice was

prevalent. There was only one rule that Daddy gave me about Z.T. I was not to go down to Z.T.'s house on a Saturday night. From our house I could hear lots of people, loud music, laughter, and what seemed like a most wonderful party. However, I was instructed not to go near, not even to observe. One afternoon I asked my dad for an explanation. I told Daddy I knew Z.T. wouldn't hurt me or let anybody else hurt me. My dad chuckled and made a joke. I laughed, although I did not really understand, and knew he would not diminish Z.T. with further explanation.

For years my dad had been the business manager at the Griffin Laundry, but the owners of the laundry were retiring, and it was closing. All his life Daddy had wanted to have either a restaurant of his own or a grocery store of his own. Mama had said, "Oh, no, you are not going to have your daughter and me waiting on tables. We do that enough at home!" Consequently, Daddy opened Westmoreland's Self-Service Grocery. In the fifth grade I was working part-time as a cashier in the store. My mom did the bookkeeping, my brother bagged and carried out groceries, and my dad was the butcher. Z.T. stocked the shelves and helped cook because, you see, my dad had not completely let go of the restaurant idea.

Since he loved to cook, Daddy and Z.T. spent hours preparing a variety of items that were sold in the store – barbeque sauce, chicken salad, brunswick stew, pimiento cheese, and souse meat. Z.T. made souse meat by the bucketfuls, and it sold like hotcakes. Daddy always molded it into a loaf, refrigerated it, sliced it perfectly, and put it in the meat counter next to the specialty meats like caviar. It was years later when I was invited to an elegant occasion at Hilton Head Island, where I was introduced to paté for the first time, that I noticed the striking resemblance between the expensive delicacy and the souse meat. With a burst of unexplained laughter, I could only envision how many people passing through town might have bought and served Z.T.'s souse meat thinking that it was paté.

It never occurred to me, until the store opened, that Z.T. didn't finish school or that he didn't know how to read. As he stocked the shelves he looked at the pictures on the cans, related them to the words, and taught himself. Daddy gave him extra instruction as they worked together but always did it in private so as not to demean him. Everyone who shopped at the store grew to love Z.T. He was always smiling, was so good natured, and was so full of inner joy. His cheerfulness made you want to be around him.

For me, Z.T. grew to represent security. As a teenager it became my job to cut the grass at our house. When the lawn mower quit, I'd call my dad at the store, and he'd say, "You need oil in the mower. Call Z.T., and ask him to show you how to add oil." If I had car trouble, he would say, "Call Z.T., and ask him to come to the store so I can come help you." Z.T. was too young to be a father image to me and too helpful to be like a big brother. He was just Z.T. – a special person in everyone's life.

As the store opened one Monday morning, Z.T. showed up at the front door all cut up with multiple knife wounds. Z.T. told Daddy he had made a woman mad Saturday night, and she had come after him with a butcher knife. That was the weekend that Z.T. got religion. My dad doctored him up and talked to him a good long while. It seemed to be a turning point in both men's lives. The number of Saturday night parties decreased significantly after that.

Decades later I was having a group of teachers come to my home in metro-Atlanta for a brunch on the day after Christmas. One looked at a photo collage on the wall and asked, "Who is that black man you are with in the photo?" I replied, "That's Z.T. I put his picture out with all the family photos." Through the years Z.T. had become more than a friend to my dad and the rest of us. He had become family. He had married and had children. Each Christmas morning, after opening gifts at home, my dad would go to Z.T.'s house and play Santa Claus for his children. What a joy it was for both men!

When my dad became terminally ill with cancer, Z.T. was as pained as the rest of us. When he became confined to bed, Daddy spent days giving both Z.T. and me instructions about how to care for my mom and the farm once he was gone. He gave most of his clothes to Z.T. Daddy told Z.T. to call me after he died if he ever needed anything. We had never discussed emotions, but Daddy knew that I loved Z.T. because he was always there for my family.

Daddy died. My heart ripped in two. Z.T. understood. His heart ripped in two as well. My mother had lost down to ninety pounds during his illness and was frail. For the next four years Z.T. worked in a grocery store in town as a butcher. Daddy had taught him how to cut meat in the store so that the load could be shared. Every day after work, Z.T. would drive into Mother's yard, pull his car even with the back door, and blow the car horn. Mama would be sitting at the kitchen table. She would wave at him to let him know she was okay. Then he would go home. Living out of town, I received great comfort knowing that Z.T. chose to minister to my mother in this way.

Mother rented out the pastures for cattle ranching after Daddy died, and for the next four years Z.T. took care of anything on the farm that was not covered in the lease, judging for himself what was needed. His children had called my parents Grandmama and Grandpapa. After Daddy was gone, Z.T. began referring to my dad as Papa and my mom as Mama. It was comforting. Each Christmas I would send Z.T. a check in the same amount that my dad had always given me at Christmas time. I knew I couldn't replace my dad as Santa Claus to Z.T.'s children. Somehow, though, helping financially and trying to let him know I was there if he needed help seemed to make the pain of the loss more tolerable. Z.T. was always so appreciative.

Mama was eventually diagnosed with lung cancer like my dad. She had only a few months to live. Z.T. and I were both there for her and for each other. She died. Z.T. sat with the family at the funeral. He mourned as one of us.

I had always thought that Z.T. would be around to take care of the farm after both of my parents were gone, but Z.T. had been sick during my mom's illness and went to a doctor after she died. He was diagnosed with lung cancer, too. The chemotherapy and radiation did not help. In the hospital he said to me, "I can't work, and there is no way for us to pay the gas company for heat or pay the insurance on our car. Will you help us?" It was the first time Z.T. had ever asked me for anything. With tears and gratitude I wrote checks to the gas company and insurance company. I cleared the refrigerator, freezer, and pantry and took food to them. I gave them furniture from the house that they could sell and checked with them regularly to see if there was anything they needed.

It was only a few short months after my mom passed away that Z.T. died. His family invited me to sit with them at the funeral. I was honored. The church was packed. Z.T. had become a deacon in his later years, and the congregation felt its loss.

There had been times when I had pondered what life would be like without my parents and had attempted to prepare myself as much as one can for their transition into the next life. However, it had never occurred to me that someday I might lose Z.T. I was shattered and totally unprepared for the pain that ensued. It had been easy to talk to people about the loss of my parents and to receive understanding and compassion over that loss. I was limited, though, in the number of people in front of whom I could express such grief for this black man who had been a lifetime friend and have it truly understood. A silent suffering followed.

My mind jumped back to the playground where the little white boy and the little black boy were playing joyfully together at recess so soon after integration had come to the southern schools. It had been in that moment that I knew that my ministry in life was to be an elementary school teacher. I had never planned to teach school, but God had placed me where I could do the most good and teach others the lessons that my dad and Z.T. had taught me already, and were still to teach me until their deaths, not so much by their words but by their actions. You don't have to be a certain color to love or to be loved. You don't have to be a particular race to need or to be needed. We're all just folks, and Christ's message is for us all.

But when the Pharisees heard that he had silenced the Sadducees, they came together.

And one of them, a lawyer, asked him a question, to test him. "Teacher, which is the great commandment in the law?" And he said to him, "You shall love the Lord your God with all your heart, and with all your soul, and with all your mind. This is the great and first commandment.

And a second is like it, You shall love your neighbor as yourself. On these two commandments depend all the law and the prophets."

MATTHEW 22:34–40

A new commandment I give to you, that you love one another; even as I have loved you, that you also love one another. By this all men will know that you are my disciples, if you have love for one another."

JOHN 13:34–35

Owe no one anything, except to love one another; for he who loves his neighbor has fulfilled the law.

The commandments, "You shall not commit adultery, You shall not kill, You shall not steal, You shall not covet," and any other commandment, are summed up in this sentence, "You shall love your neighbor as yourself."

Love does no wrong to a neighbor; therefore love is the fulfilling of the law.

ROMANS 13:8–10

And Peter opened his mouth and said:
"Truly I perceive that God shows no partiality,
but in every nation
any one who fears him and does what is right
is acceptable to him."

ACTS 10:34–35

Prayer

Heavenly Father, we give thanks for the opportunities that come our way to love others. Keep us reminded that prejudice is inconsistent with Your commandment to love one another. We acknowledge that love does no wrong to a neighbor and that love represents the fulfilling of the law. We accept that we are not made worthy because of our skin color, our gender, our nationality, our education, or our social status. It is through Your grace and mercy that we have been made worthy in a way that cannot be achieved on our own, and we thank You for this blessing. We ask for Your assistance in remembering that all who fear You as the one true God, and who attempt to do what is right, are acceptable in Your sight.

FIVE

A Loved One's Suicide Attempt

It was Thanksgiving Day many years ago when I dropped by his home and found him sitting alone at the kitchen table, intoxicated, waving a pistol, and threatening to kill himself. He had been like a father to me, a brother, and a best friend for a lifetime. As a child I remembered watching him as a deacon in the church serving communion to the believers and was shocked when he turned to a bottle for relief from life's problems. Seasonal depression and alcohol abuse had interfered with many of his relationships throughout the next few decades.

He had no problem quitting the drinking cold turkey once he made his mind up to do so and typically remained sober during the spring and summer months. Those were the months when he made others laugh, restored ties with his family, and was there to help anyone in need. You would not have known he was the same person in the fall and winter when a dreary gloom affected both his life and, consequently, the lives of those who loved him. He was like Dr. Jekyll and Mr. Hyde. His family and friends knew to stay out of his way and simply weather the storm as a means of survival.

Going for counseling was considered a weakness by his

generation, not a strength, and no one was familiar with the term "Seasonal Affective Disorder" or spoke much about antidepressants. The family doctor was a person you visited every few decades if you were seriously ill, so his doctor was not aware of the problem, and the church became the enemy through the distortion of the bottle. There was no longer an interest in church attendance, spiritual enlightenment, or prayer. It had been my experience that there was little I could do for him during those times except to say I would be praying for him, that I cared for him, and would visit again at a better time.

However, on that Thanksgiving Day I knew that he would not survive without intervention. Never had the depression been that severe. His wife of many years had gone to stay with a relative out of state for her own emotional survival, and other relatives had withdrawn in desperation as well. They had done their best for him but recognized it was not enough. Self-preservation became their only option following numerous attempts to rescue him from self-destruction. Over the next few weeks he called me on more than one occasion in the middle of the night, intoxicated, and declared his intention to end his life. More than once I drove nearly 100 miles in the middle of the night to stop him. With the pressure of a full-time teaching career, family, and other responsibilities, I was becoming less and less effective in every area of my life. I had prayed diligently and found strength for my own life through the church, but the feelings of helplessness and exhaustion from the failure of this situation became overwhelming. A clinical psychologist was consulted to obtain information on pattern drinking and the legalities involved in committing someone for care.

It was late on a Friday night, shortly after Thanksgiving, when his last phone call came threatening suicide. I was sick, running a fever, getting behind with my work, and had personal problems that were pulling me down. His wife had returned home and had retreated to the back of the house as she often did during his drinking stints. All I could say was that I could not make the drive up to help him, to please go to bed and sleep it off, and that I would pray for him. He hung up on me in anger.

Typically I would call him back when that happened, but that night I did not. That night I prayerfully commended the problem to God's care and fell into a deep sleep from exhaustion. That night this person, who had been such an integral part of my life for so many years, shot himself in the head. It was two days later when his wife called and told me he had survived the gunshot wound and was in a detoxification center. She said that after he had hung up on me, and while I was praying for him, he put the pistol to his head but looked down at the phone in hopeful anticipation that I would call back. Just at the moment that his head dropped to look at the phone, which he claimed later to be ringing, he pulled the trigger. The tilt of his head caused the bullet to miss his brain. The doctor said the phone call had saved his life. His wife told me, however, that none of the phones in the house ever rang.

He asked me at the detoxification center, "You called me back, didn't you?" I could not bring myself to tell him that I had not because he would have been so crushed. I just said, "I've been so sick that I hardly even remember the weekend, but I prayed for you after you hung up and commended the problem to God's care." I continued, "I love you, but you have a problem that I can no longer endure, so I will continue to put it in God's hands. If you ever take another drink, I will never come to visit you again because I love you too much to watch you destroy yourself." I hugged this most special person and his wife and left.

He never took another drink. In addition to physical healing and plastic surgery, he took antidepressants for awhile and went for counseling. I visited more frequently than ever to ensure support. He lived the next fifteen years in total sobriety and died of natural causes. On his death bed he confirmed to me that he believed in Jesus as the Son of God and said he would be waiting for me in heaven to help me make the transition from this life to the next when my time came, but he just had one more thing to ask of me. He asked me to be there for his wife when he was gone in the way that I had been there for him. I promised I would and was at her bedside when she passed away. Her death certificate listed heart failure as the cause, but one doctor suggested that she grieved herself to death. She and her husband had endured life's good times and its trials together for over fifty years. They lived in a time when divorce was neither fashionable nor acceptable, and they learned to overcome problems through trust and endurance.

Every Thanksgiving I thank God for the lessons I have learned from my failures in life because it has been at those times that I have turned everything over to Him and have grown stronger in the faith. Trust is essential.

In God,
whose word I praise,
in God
I trust without a fear.
What can flesh do to me?

PSALM 56:4

Trust in the Lord
with all your heart,
and do not rely
on your own insight.

PROVERBS 3:5

For thus said the Lord God,
the Holy One of Israel,
"In returning and rest you shall be saved;
in quietness
and in trust shall be your strength."

ISAIAH 30:15

Many are the pangs of the wicked;
but steadfast love
surrounds him who trusts in the Lord.

PSALM 32:10

Blessed is the man
who makes the Lord his trust,
who does not turn
to the proud, to those who go astray
after false gods!

PSALM 40:4

Prayer

Heavenly Father, we praise You for being there for us at times when we feel so helpless. Give us the strength and the discipline to trust in You more fully in times of crisis. Keep us reminded that reading Your word, praying, and spending time with other believers can keep us renewed and refreshed as we face the problems before us. Protect us from the unhealthy choices and addictions that tempt us when our guard is down. Forgive us of our failures during those times. We accept that Your promises go unchanged and that our faith can sustain us through all.

SIX

When the Church Uplifts You –
My Own Brush with Death

It was a crisp, sunny day in mid-December, and I was driving down Highway 16 on the way back to Griffin without a hint that my life was about to change. Christmas carols were playing on the radio, and thoughts of further shopping prevailed when a nausea attack hit without warning. Assuming it was the virus that had been running rampant in the area, the decision was made to go straight home. However, the urge for relief became so intense that I pulled over on the side of the road, opened the car door, and began heaving without time to even release the seatbelt.

Feeling weakened, but still in control, I stepped carefully out of the car with cell phone in hand. Walking to less offensive ground, I dropped to my knees and collapsed in the grass, massaging the middle of my back for what was assumed to be a muscle spasm caused from twisting in the closely bound seatbelt. It did not really seem like a crisis at the time. However, I phoned two friends and left brief messages that I had stopped on the side of the road sick and may need some help. They had been repeatedly coached, if anything ever happened to me, to

65

go get my pet – a twelve-year-old dachshund that had been with me since he was eight weeks old. He was both my companion and my child, asleep in an oversized crate inside the house with impaired vision and faulty hearing. Surely I would be able to get up and go home to care for us both, but I was taught to always look ahead and to stay on the safe side. What I did not know was that, due to the violent retching, my esophagus had ripped. My last meal, consumed only a short time before, had begun slowly emptying into my chest cavity and left lung.

It seemed strange that so many cars kept passing by without anyone stopping. Griffin was known to be somewhat racially challenged, but it was an African-American who stopped to help me. It reminded me of the story of the Good Samaritan in which the "enemy" stopped to help a person in need while friendly factions avoided the scene. He asked if I needed him to call an ambulance, and I declined. "I know this looks terrible," I blurted out, "a black man bent over a white woman, but I seem to have a muscle spasm in my back. If you would just reach around and rub the middle of my back I believe the spasm might stop so I can drive home." Like any other stranger, he could have taken my car or the purse that remained on the front seat or not even have stopped at all. However, this kind man massaged the middle of my back in a most gentlemanly fashion for a few moments until the pain subsided and escorted me back to my car. He offered to follow me to the hospital, but I assured him it was just a virus and a back problem, not realizing it was much more.

Before getting home, the pain struck again, this time more severely than before. I stopped by the chiropractor's office for an adjustment for what I continued to believe was a muscle spasm, and the doctor immediately realized that there was something more serious that needed attention. She asked her receptionist to drive me to the nearest emergency clinic. Bent over double on the floorboard of the back seat of the van, I managed to call back one of the friends who was phoned earlier. She was already on the way to the hospital. Personnel at the clinic could not ease the pain and called an ambulance to transport me to the local emergency room.

A second friend was on the way by the time I arrived at the hospital. The doctor dropped everything to focus on my condition, correctly diagnosed the problem, and arranged for surgery in Atlanta. He had me placed on a helicopter unconscious and on life support. My friends were told that there was no guarantee I would survive the flight. They were instructed that, if I did arrive alive, there was a chance I might not survive the surgery – that 30% of the people who have that type of surgery do not live through it. As the helicopter lifted in the midnight hour, my friends got in their cars and drove to Atlanta, but not before getting one of their husbands to go get my pet. The surgeon asked my friends what kind of constitution I had before beginning surgery. "She is a fighter," one said. "She is a fighter!" The surgeon gave instructions to proceed. My friends remained throughout the night, exhausted and worried.

A day had been lost before my eyes opened slowly in the dimly lit Intensive Care Unit of the Atlanta hospital where a male nurse stood with his back to me as he gazed into a computer. I was still on life support and could hardly move. There were no familiar faces in the room, and I had no memory of the ambulance ride to the local emergency room or of the hours spent at the hospital in Atlanta. "Was I in an accident?" The nurse responded with surprise and compassion, "Don't you remember?" He went on to explain, "Your esophagus ripped. You were life-flighted to Atlanta for emergency surgery." I fell back to sleep.

My eyes opened a second time. There was no concept of how much time had passed. A female nurse was now gazing into the computer. There was no one else in the room. I asked, "Will you call my minister?" The nurse responded abruptly, "No. There will be plenty of time for that later." My mind shifted to a sermon I had heard years earlier in which the minister insisted that God knows what we need before we ever ask for it and how He will provide. I fell asleep again.

My eyes opened a third time, again with no concept of how much time had passed. This time a kind hand touched my left arm, and a young nurse whispered, "I just wanted to tell you that your church in Griffin called. They wanted you to know that they love you and that they are praying for you." I smiled and knew that God had provided. At that moment I knew I would be all right. First Baptist would send out an e-mail asking for prayer. It would be forwarded all over town and outside of town. I had always been a big believer in prayer and knew its power.

Using sign language, I let the nurse know I wanted to write something. She handed me pen and paper on which I scribbled the name and phone number of a Christian friend in Atlanta who was contacted and who stayed with me until I was moved to a room where two friends from Forsyth awaited with sighs of relief and welcome smiles.

The medication was so strong that I had yet to realize that I had been cut up the front, cut across the back, had two hoses in my left side, had one hose in my right side, had two tubes coming out of my stomach, and was attached to two IVs. The next ten days were filled with pain, agitation, frustration, and aggravation. I could not get out of bed without help or move around the room without a wheeled cart to carry the mass of mechanical attachments. I could not bathe myself completely and was not allowed to swallow anything, not even a few drops of water, for the first seven days. A small, wet sponge was provided to soothe my parched tongue and chapped lips. Some of the nurses were empathetic, and others appeared negligent. The hospital was understaffed, and I was not a good patient.

A friend who is a minister called from Virginia and listened to me emote. She knew that my parents were deceased, that I had never had children, and that my husband was gone. She knew that I never referred to myself as being alone because I knew otherwise but that I needed to regain my focus. "Jane," she said sternly, "People will hurt you. They will abandon you and betray you, but God is on His throne and is sitting right next to you. Focus on Him! Focus on Him!" I began to think more about the friends who had spent so many hours at the hospital awaiting my surgery, the ministers who were visiting me, the friends who were driving through Atlanta traffic from several cities to let me know they cared, and the testimony I might be able to share if I actually survived the hospital experience.

After ten days in the hospital they sent me home. I don't think they released me. I think they evicted me. It was the day before Christmas Eve when the staples were removed from my front and back. I still could walk only a short distance, could not bathe without help, could consume only liquids, and would have two tubes remain in my stomach for an additional two weeks. The doctor said that recovery would take three to six months but that I should never have problems with my esophagus again. He described it as a freak accident to a healthy esophagus.

My surgeon had told me that I would be sent home with bandages and instructions for cleaning and dressing the area where the two tubes protruded, along with his phone numbers if I had questions. However, he was not on duty when I left, and there were no bandages or phone numbers supplied or instructions about the tubes. Questions about whether or not I needed to hire a nurse or ask someone to stay with me had gone unanswered or had been answered too vaguely to draw conclusions. I had been sent home in such haste that there had not been time to formulate other essential questions. The paperwork sent with me said not to lift heavy items, not to go swimming for three weeks, and to call for an appointment to have tubes removed. I could have figured that much out on my own.

I should have been grateful. They had saved my life. I was not grateful. I was angry because my independence had been taken away. I was fearful because I did not know what quality of life to expect or how to deal with the situation at hand. I was frustrated and confused by the narcotic that eased the physical agony but prohibited problem-solving skills from functioning. Within the first twenty-four hours I was home there were forty phone calls and twelve visitors. Getting up and down to take calls and answer the door was more than could be physically handled. Emotionally I could not share with friends in the rejoicing of a life saved. The pain was excruciating. I lived alone, could not drive, and would be at other people's mercy without a clue of how long. My pet could not come home because I could not care for him. Solid foods were to remain off limits for another week until liquids could be replaced by homemade baby food. I could not talk without gasping for air and had to sleep in a reclined position on the sofa.

Depression had begun to set in. I stayed up most of the night my first day home, watching the clock, not wanting to impose on anyone too early in the morning. Before the sun was up I called a neighbor who was the Minister of Education at church and told him I could not do this alone and did not have enough medical knowledge to know how to help myself. He came to see me just before Sunday School that morning, listened to my concerns, and sent a church member who was a nurse. She brought bandages and tape, taught me how to dress the wounds, and assisted me with bathing until I could do it myself.

Over the next three and a half months my Sunday School class, Homeowners' Association, and other friends literally adopted me. My Sunday School class organized a list of names and phone numbers and times they could help if I would call or e-mail to let them know what was needed. They were available to me on a daily basis throughout my recovery and brought my first meals of pureed vegetables. The minister gave spiritual support, specifically recommending that I read all of the Psalms without skipping the angry ones. The church sent deacons to administer communion, and cards of encouragement came in the mail daily. Church members read the

Bible to me, prayed for me, and gave words of encouragement regarding progress made. The Homeowners' Association also organized meals that were brought in and provided help on short notice as well. Both local and out-of-town friends were there each time there was a need. God loves us through other people, and He sent a multitude of them to deliver groceries and prescriptions, to bring food, to take me to doctor appointments both in town and in Atlanta, to run errands, and to assist with housework.

There were physical setbacks – a cold with a persistent cough, an infection that warranted a trip to the emergency room in Atlanta, inflamed tissue that formed, and reactions to medications. However, over the weeks my anger faded because of the love that was received. I asked God to forgive my attitude and gave Him thanks for sparing my life. I gave thanks for the church members and other friends and neighbors who all joined together to keep me spiritually, physically, and emotionally nourished during the healing process. With the gratitude that came, I confessed the acknowledgment that I was spared for a purpose and gave a commitment to seek out God's will for fulfilling it. It had always been easy for me to be a giver, but being a receiver was not so simple. I truly learned the value of friendship, how to be vulnerable, how to open up, how to connect, and how to receive love.

After three and a half months I was able to get off of the narcotic prescribed for pain, shifted to milder medications, and was able to drive again. My first drive was to Physical Therapy, the second was to the pharmacy, and the third was to Wal-Mart where I equated walking the aisles to a summer vacation. I was able to care for my pet again and rejoiced at having him home. Sleeping in bed for the first time in months was a special luxury. Cooking and cleaning house became a joyful part of the daily routine because I could do it myself. The physical therapist taught me exercises that took forty-five minutes twice a day in order to assist with scar tissue stiffness, joint problems that had set in from the sedentary lifestyle of recovery, and weakness that had resulted from losing twenty pounds along with a great deal of muscle tone. Within a few weeks the doctors and therapists dismissed me with instructions to continue exercises on my own. As my independence was restored, however, my dependence upon God remained deepened.

Prayer remained an important part of every day. Writing also resumed its place as part of the day. After retiring from teaching in the public school system, I had worked as a part-time news writer for a local radio station and occasionally contributed editorials for the local newspaper. For years friends had encouraged me to write a book which had been started, and now my commitment to that endeavor was heightened. Writing down life's experiences and the scriptures that had sustained me through those experiences provided purpose. It was felt that those stories might help others in their personal spiritual journeys and might have the potential to further someone else's healing and hope.

We are put on this earth to love one another and to help one another. How others treat us is out of our control a good bit of the time. However, the decision to love God and obey His word is very much in our control. The decision to accept Christ as His Son and as a Savior is very much in our control. The decision to allow God's light to shine through the Holy Spirit that dwells within us is very much in our control. We have the ability to overcome life's tragedies because God provides the tools to do so if we just ask and plod on with determination. We may become lonely, but we are never alone. God remains on His throne. He remains faithful to us, and His promises remain unchanged.

The Good Samaritan

And behold, a lawyer stood up to put him to the test, saying, "Teacher, what shall I do to inherit eternal life?" He said to him, "What is written in the law? How do you read?" And he answered, "You shall love the Lord your God with all your heart, and with all your soul, and with all your strength, and with all your mind; and your neighbor as yourself." And he said to him, "You have answered right; do this, and you will live."

But he, desiring to justify himself, said to Jesus, "And who is my neighbor?"

Jesus replied, "A man was going down from Jerusalem to Jericho, and he fell among robbers, who stripped him and beat him, and departed, leaving him half dead. Now by chance a priest was going down that road; and when he saw him he passed by on the other side. So likewise a Levite, when he came to the place and saw him, passed by on the other side. But a Samaritan, as he journeyed, came to where he was; and when he saw him, he had compassion, and went to him and bound up his wounds, pouring on oil and wine; then he set him on his own beast and brought him to an inn, and took care of him. And the next day he took out two denarii and gave them to the innkeeper, saying, 'Take care of him; and whatever more you spend, I will repay you when I come back.'

Which of these three, do you think, proved neighbor to the man who fell among the robbers?" He said, "The one who showed mercy on him."

And Jesus said to him, "Go and do likewise."

LUKE 10:25–37

Love

If I speak in the tongues of men and of angels, but have not love, I am a noisy gong or a clanging cymbal. And if I have prophetic powers, and understand all mysteries and all knowledge, and if I have all faith, so as to remove mountains, but have not love, I am nothing. If I give away all I have, and if I deliver my body to be burned, but have not love, I gain nothing.

Love is patient and kind; love is not jealous or boastful; it is not arrogant or rude. Love does not insist on its own way; it is not irritable or resentful; it does not rejoice at wrong, but rejoices in the right. Love bears all things, believes all things, hopes all things, endures all things.

Love never ends; as for prophecies, they will pass away; as for tongues, they will cease; as for knowledge, it will pass away. For our knowledge is imperfect and our prophecy is imperfect; but when the perfect comes, the imperfect will pass away. When I was a child, I spoke like a child, I thought like a child, I reasoned like a child; when I became a man, I gave up childish ways. For now we see in a mirror dimly, but then face to face. Now I know in part; then I shall understand fully, even as I have been fully understood.

So faith, hope, love abide, these three; but the greatest of these is love.

1 CORINTHIANS, CHAPTER 13

More than that,
we rejoice in our sufferings,
knowing that suffering produces endurance,
and endurance produces character,
and character produces hope,
and hope does not disappoint us,
because God's love
has been poured into our hearts
through the Holy Spirit
which has been given to us.

ROMANS 5:3–5

As he passed by,
he saw a man blind from his birth.

And his disciples asked him,
"Rabbi, who sinned, this man or his parents,
that he was born blind?"

Jesus answered,
"It was not that this man sinned, or his parents,
but that the works of God
might be made manifest in him."

JOHN 9:1–3

Prayer

Heavenly Father, we give thanks for the good Samaritans of our day who stop to help us when others pass by. We come to You in gratitude for the many ways that You love us through others. We give thanks for Your instruction on love that allows us to be used as Your tools. Help us to love with more patience and kindness. Remove any jealousy, boastfulness, arrogance, or rudeness in our hearts because we know it spills over into our speech and actions. Give us the self-discipline to refrain from insisting on our own way. Help us to control any irritability or resentfulness in our lives and to rejoice in that which is right. Allow us to accept that our sufferings bring endurance which leads to character and ultimately produces hope. Thank You for our health that allows us to serve You. May our thoughts, our words, and our actions truly glorify You.

SEVEN

When the Church Lets You Down — A Story of Stewardship

Her biggest trial in the area of forgiveness involved being hurt by a minister whom she had respected and trusted over several years. Under his leadership she found herself engulfed in meaningful worship services, attending Wednesday night suppers, enjoying a ladies' study group, and directing Vacation Bible School for over 200 children. She had moved to that city for professional reasons, had no biological family there, and the church served as her family of choice. There was great sorrow when another move became necessary, but she knew that sometimes God moves us when we want to stay still.

A couple of years had passed when she heard that the pastor of that church, who had been there for over two decades, had left under very unpleasant circumstances. The elders had asked for his resignation. The church had split, and a small group of members were encouraging the minister to start a new church. She reflected on how his sermons had fed her spiritually at a time when she was in great need and how much she had appreciated his counseling in a time of personal crisis. Dealings with him had never been unpleasant. Feeling

78

called to remain removed from whatever had happened and to be supportive, she became one of the backers of the new church. Funds that had been recently inherited were donated to provide rent for the new church for the first year. A second donation was made that would allow the purchase of enough land to build a church. God appeared to be working through her to help an unemployed minister who had once helped her. However, the giving experience turned into a nightmare.

The minister had been asked to keep her donations anonymous, but several people in the new church volunteered that he had betrayed her trust by personally confiding the name of the donor. The Bible said to confront one who offends us, so she asked him. He denied it.

Along with the request for anonymity there had been a request to receive a monthly account of how much money was coming into the church, how much was going out, and where it was going. She was assured both by the Finance Committee and by the minister that her request would be honored and assumed it to be a simple task since the only expenses were rent, the minister's salary, and a few supplies for a congregation of fewer than 30 people. However, after six months of operation, the church still provided no monthly financial reports in spite of repeated requests. Finance Committee members were consumed with their own stresses of life and passed the buck. Since elders had not been elected, the minister was considered the Chief Elder and highest official. It was an independent church with no higher earthly authority to require accountability. He was the only paid employee, but when she went to him for help, he told her he did not involve himself in finances. A member of the Finance Committee who worked at the bank where the church did business told her, however, that the minister came in weekly to ask for cashier's checks from the church's bank account to pay himself and for reimbursement of supplies.

The church had begun services in the fall. She went to the minister in mid-February for a receipt for donations for tax purposes when the Finance Committee produced none. He responded with intense anger, again claiming that he did not get involved with finances, but eventually typed one for her.

Her donations were made only after the minister had confirmed that the church had been incorporated and had a tax identification number. However, in March he announced to the congregation that the church was not incorporated after all and that an attorney had been hired to assist with that. He explained that the church had been doing business with cashier's checks over past months because they could not write checks off of their own account until incorporated. He assured the congregation business would be handled.

She became ill and did not attend for weeks. The minister did not contact her. Then, one day he called and asked if he and his wife could take her out to dinner and pick up a keyboard she had offered to donate earlier. It was hoped that there would be a productive visit, but the minister had a temper outburst in the restaurant that left both his wife and her sitting at the table crying. The outburst was caused when she asked when monthly financial statements would be provided and what the problems were with incorporation. He took her back home, dinner untouched, where his anger level flared again with no apparent provocation. This time he suggested that the church just return the money she had donated for land. Feeling terribly offended by that offer, she tearfully declined, telling him all she wanted was simple financial accountability, not a refund.

It was a sleepless night, and questions bombarded her mind. The next day she made a phone call to the Secretary of State's office to ask what was preventing the church's incorporation, to the Internal Revenue Service to see if there was a tax identification number for the church that would make members' donations deductible, and to an officer of the bank where the church did business to find out why the church was being allowed to do business for several months using cashier's checks. The Secretary of State's office provided documentation that the church had been incorporated since the previous November with the minister listed as the agent. The IRS indicated that the church was doing business under two slightly different names and had a tax identification number under only one of those names. They could not tell her which one because she was not a corporate officer. An officer at the bank shared that the minister had been told not to come in there for any more cashier's checks–to take care of business as explained to him previously so that checks could be written off of the church's account.

She was devastated emotionally and spiritually by what was happening. Her respect for the minister had crumbled, and she no longer experienced that church as a "safe" place to attend. She wanted to chalk the whole thing up as an error in judgment on her part, find another church home, and put the ordeal behind her. However, it was as though God kept nudging her through the sleepless nights with a job that she simply did not want.

Finally, her accountant and attorney were consulted regarding the legality of tax returns. Two ministers and a Christian counselor were consulted for guidance in handling the matter with biblical principles while keeping herself protected.

The two ministers and the counselor, none of whom knew each other or had any contact with each other, all made reference to the same two scriptures. The first required that Christians not sue a brother in Christ because of how it would look for the church in front of nonbelievers. The second described the steps to be taken when the church's leaders did not follow biblical procedures. Those steps included truthful confrontation, the presentation of witnesses if that did not work, and congregational enlightenment as a last resort.

To avoid further confrontation, she handled the matter in writing over the next several months. A request was sent to the minister and Finance Committee asking for monthly financial statements that were promised, but they never came. A letter was then sent to the church accepting the minister's offer to return the funds donated for land in lieu of providing financial accountability. That resulted in the receipt of an unsigned letter, church financial records for three months, copies of bank statements for three months that did not match those records, and a church newsletter that contradicted both. A subsequent letter requesting clarification was sent and was ignored except that she was taken off of the church's mailing list for future newsletters.

A month later, a letter was sent from her attorney requesting clarification and monthly financial statements. The attorney's letter was ignored. Finally, a letter went to the congregation documenting events. It included copies of statements from three church members who had withdrawn their membership stating that it was due to problems with the minister and/or because of the way that business was being conducted. Finally, with no response, she withdrew her membership and requested that the name of the family from whom she had inherited the funds not be used in conjunction with that church's name, as the funds had been donated in their memory. Upon receiving her membership withdrawal, the minister sent an e-mail telling her that any further communication from her would be erased or deleted.

Then two contacts were made that indicated a change in heart. First, her attorney received a pre-dated letter from the minister with an attempt at financial accountability. Enclosed were back issues of all the newsletters that he had denied her. The second was a contact by the church's attorney stating that they wanted to return the money donated for land as suggested by the minister. It seems that a church member had called a congregational meeting on her behalf after membership was withdrawn and had insisted on action to make the situation right.

However, months went by, and all that was ever received were excuses. The church member who had called the congregational meeting confided that he and his family were leaving that church, as had many others. The church's attorney refused to represent them further when they did not return the money as promised through him. Upon further contact, the minister sent a letter that the funds he had offered to return would not be returned then or ever. He said it was because she had had contact with members of their congregation that was against an agreement made. No such agreement was ever made to that effect or could be made. A standard release form was to be signed upon receipt of funds, but that never happened.

It had become clear that the issue was one of control, not resolution. She had wanted financial accountability and was accepting the funds the minister offered to return only in lieu of that, but it was clear she was to receive neither.

The biblical response at that point was simply to pray for them. She did not want to, but other ministers insisted that her heart would eventually catch up with her mind if she did the right thing.

She prayed. She prayed for God's church, for the leaders who betray God's trust, and for the members who leave for good because of the hurt inflicted. She prayed that she would rise above the situation and use it as a learning experience.

The issue in her mind had less to do with finances than with how we treat our fellow human beings. It was an issue of honesty, respect, consideration, and appreciation. It was an issue about using age-old biblical instruction in dealing with today's problems. It was an issue of dealing with personal temptation – the temptation to deal unproductively with the stress inflicted upon her, to drop out of church, to obsess over the injustice of it all, and to treat others as she had been treated. It was a time when her heart was tempted to become hard and a time when there ceased to be joy in giving.

She spent time reflecting on the pain and how the situation might have been handled differently. Then she crossed paths with a friend from her church home from years before who summed it all up in one simple statement: "The Devil is picking on you because he perceives you as such a threat." Another friend insisted that she move her thinking away from the principles that others should be following, and spend energy evaluating what it was that God was wanting her to do that Satan was preventing. She prayed more diligently, found herself a new church home, and hardly thought about the ordeal further. She resolved within herself that there is nothing more precious to God than His church and that He will handle any who mistreat His children or misappropriate the gifts made to further His will. She gave thanks for the lessons learned through the experience:

† God expects us to give because we are called to give, not because we will get something in return, even if the expectation is to receive the same level of respect and consideration after the gift as before. We have already been rewarded for our gifts through God's grace, His love, and the sacrifice of His Son for our awakening.

† God can't use our money any more than He could use the animal sacrifices or agricultural tithes of ancient believers. Our gifts are an expression of the depth of our love and faith that we are offering Him. They are a gesture of gratitude for what we have received, not a manipulative technique designed to gain more blessings.

† A church is not built with money. You can pay rent to hold services and call it a church. You can buy land, and build a structure, and give it a church name. However, if God's love does not radiate from those inside its walls, and biblical principles are ignored, it is of little use to God. His church is within people, and His love is not confined by walls.

† Vengeance belongs to God, not to humans.

† Satan comes after those who are a threat to his mission. If you really intend to help build God's kingdom, fasten your seatbelt. It is going to be a bumpy ride.

God Loves a Cheerful Giver

The point is this: he who sows sparingly will also reap sparingly, and he who sows bountifully will also reap bountifully. Each one must do as he has made up his mind, not reluctantly or under compulsion, for God loves a cheerful giver. And God is able to provide you with every blessing in abundance, so that you may always have enough of everything and may provide in abundance for every good work.

2 CORINTHIANS 9:6–8

Pastoral Duties to Elders

Let the elders who rule well be considered worthy of double honor, especially those who labor in preaching and teaching; for the scripture says, "You shall not muzzle an ox when it is treading out the grain, and, "The laborer deserves his wages."

Never admit any charge against an elder except on the evidence of two or three witnesses. As for those who persist in sin, rebuke them in the presence of all, so that the rest may stand in fear. In the presence of God and of Christ Jesus and of the elect angels I charge you to keep these rules without favor, doing nothing from partiality. Do not be hasty in the laying on of hands, nor participate in another man's sins; keep yourself pure.

No longer drink only water, but use a little wine for the sake of your stomach and your frequent ailments.

The sins of some men are conspicuous, pointing to judgment, but the sins of others appear later. So also good deeds are conspicuous; and even when they are not, they cannot remain hidden.

1 TIMOTHY 5:17–25

Lawsuits Among Brothers

When one of you has a grievance against a brother, does he dare go to law before the unrighteous instead of the saints? Do you not know that the saints will judge the world? And if the world is to be judged by you, are you incompetent to try trivial cases? Do you not know that we are to judge angels? How much more, matters pertaining to this life! If then you have such cases, why do you lay them before those who are least esteemed by the church? I say this to your shame. Can it be that there is no man among you wise enough to decide between members of the brotherhood, but brother goes to law against brother, and that before unbelievers?

To have lawsuits at all with one another is defeat for you. Why not rather suffer wrong? Why not rather be defrauded? But you yourselves wrong and defraud, and that even your own brethren.

1 Corinthians 6:1–8

Conduct in Relation to Men

Beloved, never avenge yourselves, but leave it to the wrath of God; for it is written, "Vengeance is mine, I will repay, says the Lord."

Romans 12:19

The Test of False Prophets

*Beware of false prophets, who come to you in sheep's cloth-
ing but inwardly are ravenous wolves. You will know them
by their fruits. Are grapes gathered from thorns, or figs from
thistles? So, every sound tree bears good fruit, but the bad
tree bears evil fruit. A sound tree cannot bear evil fruit, nor
can a bad tree bear good fruit. Every tree that does not bear
good fruit is cut down and thrown into the fire. Thus you will
know them by their fruits.*

*Not every one who says to me, "Lord, Lord," shall enter the
kingdom of heaven, but he who does the will of my Father who
is in heaven. On that day many will say to me, "Lord, Lord,
did we not prophesy in your name, and cast out demons in
your name, and do many mighty works in your name?" And
then will I declare to them, "I never knew you; depart from
me, you evildoers."*

MATTHEW 7:15–23

Warning Against False Teachers

If any one teaches otherwise and does not agree with the sound words of our Lord Jesus Christ and the teaching which accords with godliness, he is puffed up with conceit, he knows nothing; he has a morbid craving for controversy and for disputes about words, which produce envy, dissension, slander, base suspicions, and wrangling among men who are depraved in mind and bereft of the truth, imagining that godliness is a means of gain.

For the love of money is the root of all evils; it is through this craving that some have wandered away from the faith and pierced their hearts with many pangs.

I TIMOTHY 6:3–5, 10

88 *Tablets of the Heart*

Christ, the Foundation

According to the grace of God
given to me,
like a skilled master builder
I laid a foundation
and another man is building upon it.
Let each man
take care how he builds upon it.
For no other foundation can any one lay
than that which is laid,
which is
Jesus Christ.

1 CORINTHIANS 3:10–11

The Teaching About Judging Others

"Judge not,
and you will not be judged;
condemn not,
and you will not be condemned;
forgive,
and you will be forgiven;
give,
and it will be given to you;
good measure,
pressed down, shaken together, running over,
will be put into your lap.
For the measure you give
will be the measure you get back."

LUKE: 6:37–38

℣rayer

Heavenly Father, we come to You knowing that we are unworthy and that we are failing miserably in so many ways. Yet You continue to forgive us and to love us through Your grace and mercy. We pray that You would help us to maintain a cheerful attitude with our giving. Keep us reminded that all that we have is a gift from You and that what we give is an expression of our faithfulness to You. We ask that You would protect us from a love of money that seeks to destroy that which is truly meaningful. Be with the ministers and leaders of every church that they would seek to love Your children in honorable ways and to treat them with biblical integrity. Be with the members who have suffered pain within the church walls to the point of withdrawing from Christian principles or fellowship. Give them strength, insights, and healing that they may find their way back home. We ask for greater discernment that we might avoid false teachings. We ask for hearts free of vengeance. Help us to forgive.

EIGHT

Seeking God's Will

After retiring as a teacher, I found myself fighting along side of 350 neighbors to retain the agricultural atmosphere surrounding the family farm. Community meetings were held, research was conducted, attorneys were consulted, petitions were signed, and phone calls were made to commissioners. Speeches were made at Planning and Zoning meetings and County Commission meetings regarding subdivisions that might be built – one adjacent to the farm with seventy-six homes on it and another close behind it with a hundred homes. How could this be happening?

The family farm was sustained by cattle ranching. Didn't the politicians and developers know that cows occasionally got out? Didn't they comprehend the mass of traffic that the subdivisions would bring or understand the liability issues involved if a car hit a cow? Didn't they understand the impact on the school system, the danger of inadequate fire protection in the area, the already present need for more law enforcement, the pollution that impended, and the water shortage issues? Didn't they understand that the taxes paid by the residents of those homes would not cover the costs of the services that had to be provided? How many times had we explained it all in public meetings in front of officials? Politicians and developers called it progress.

After my parents had died, I had moved back to the family farm. It had been my intention to live out the rest of my life there and to be buried in the family cemetery. It had been my expectation that the man who had lived on the farm and had helped with the work would be there from then on to help me as he had my parents. However, within a short period of time he unexpectedly died.

The farm life I remembered was not my current reality. The loneliness was overwhelming, and laborers had to be secured to do the work. The pleasure in the acreage had been replaced by nonstop responsibility and constant expense for upkeep. Noise from the traffic in front of the house was worse than anything I had ever experienced in the cities where I had lived before returning home, and there was little regard for the speed limit. When I was a child, the cars literally crept down the two-lane road because people acknowledged it as an agricultural community. Everyone knew not to go over 15 miles per hour because residents had livestock that sometimes got out. Back then if someone hit your cow, they would come by the house, apologize, and offer to pay for it. Times had changed, though, and now people would simply have a lawyer contact you about damages to them or their car when they killed your animal. There were sheriff's reports to pick up the next day, insurance companies to be contacted, and your own attorney to consult. It had become a different world.

Selling the family farm became an option, and I began praying that God would let me know if I should leave the farm life behind and buy a home in town. It was a struggle.

"Lord," I prayed, "Should I consider leaving the farm? Will I be betraying family tradition and the trust of the neighbors? You know I have no children to pass it on to, no parents to enjoy it, and no husband to help me." During the next month a gas truck turned over in the front lawn, a car thief ran over the forty year old boxwood by the driveway, and a drunk driver drove through the pasture fence in the middle of the night leaving the sheriff's deputy to knock on the door to report that someone needed to be called to replace the barbed wire so that the cows could not get out.

A few more weeks went by, and I prayed, "Lord, I don't know whether or not to stay here. Can You help me know Your will for my future?" Within a few days an electrical storm blew out the television, the computer, and the answering machine.

I prayed, "Lord, if You could just give me some insight as to what it is I am to do in terms of staying on the farm or moving, I will do what You want." Another electrical storm hit. This one blew out the other television, damaged the refrigerator, and caused the light bulb under the carport to explode.

I said, "Heavenly Father, I come before You asking for guidance. I had always planned to live my final days on the family farm but am confused about what to do. Can You just give me some sign or indication of Your will?" Heavy winds blew the utility house off of its concrete slab. A fifty year old tree was blown onto the barn and crushed in the roof.

I petitioned, "Lord, is there some way that You could let me know what I am to do about this farm? It is a full time job for me just finding people to do the repairs, and my retirement check is eaten up replacing or repairing all the damages." A bolt of lightning struck a sixty year old tree causing it to fall on one end of the corral. The structure was old and collapsed to the ground.

"Lord," I said impatiently. "Why aren't You answering me? I am stressed out and do not know if I should sell the farm and move into town where I would only have a home and yard to maintain. Please help me know what to do." Over the next few weeks I discovered that the reason the water level was low in the lake was because it needed a new siphon system, and the bridge sank into what little water was underneath it.

In addition, a deer was hit by a car in front of the house and slammed into the mailbox.

I continued to replace that which was destroyed, to repair that which could be salvaged, and to have that which no longer served a purpose hauled away. With exhaustion I bowed again. "I know, Dear Father in Heaven, that You love me and that You are always there for me. However, I do not understand why there is no answer about the family farm. I am weary from the work. There is no time in my day to enjoy people or to have a life other than upkeep. What should I do? Please help me." The next week the tool house was broken into, and all of the new equipment was stolen. A water test indicated that the city's lift station was leaking sewage into the creek that ran across the pastures.

"Lord, is it possible that these things that are happening are an indication that I should move?" Within a few days the gas company indicated that the floor furnaces were leaking carbon monoxide. To make matters worse, the septic tank backed up, the tractor would not crank, and the sheriff's department had to be called about gunfire down the road in the middle of the night. Wild dogs were running rampant in the pastures, and there was evidence of trespassers.

"Heavenly Father, the repairs are almost all finished. They should hold up for the rest of my life, but I am not finding peace in my new life here. Is it okay for me to sell and move to town? I would so love to buy a home in town that I saw for sale the other day. It was everything I had ever wanted, and I would be able to see everything I owned just walking the dog around the house. The entire backyard is a showcase for nature, and it is so much quieter than where I am now. Selling the farm would free up my time to become more involved with people and to explore Your intentions for my life after retirement. Will You help me know what to do?" In the weeks to follow, county commissioners approved a subdivision to go up on one side of the farm and another to go up a short distance behind it.

"Thank You, Lord, for letting me know the answer to my prayer. I have never been hard of hearing but acknowledge that I have been hard of listening. I will try to do better. Please help the neighbors understand. Amen."

I sold the farm and moved to the city where my time was spent with people instead of with chores. It was a place where I could find joy instead of dwelling on memories of people who were no longer there. My life became enriched by church activities and new friendships, and I began writing. I was thankful for the farm experience. It gave new appreciation to the work and dedication of my family. I was equally thankful for my home in town and for a lighter load, as I learned that following God's plan and following family tradition are not always the same. There was peace in the decision.

Resurrection, I believe, is not just about the next life. It is about this life as well. It is about leaving an old life behind and starting over without letting life's defeats consume us with anger or negativity. It is about acknowledging that which brings us down and having the courage to endure the pain of the experience until we can emerge with the relief of a new life. It is about weathering the storm until we can understand the new mission. God will equip us for any job He has for us if we just seek out His will and busy ourselves following it.

I delight to do thy will,
O my God;
thy law is within my heart.

PSALM 40:8

Teach me to do thy will,
for thou art my God!
Let thy good spirit
lead me on a level path!

PSALM 143:10

And going a little farther
he fell on his face and prayed,
"My Father,
if it be possible,
let this cup pass from me;
nevertheless,
not as I will, but as thou wilt."

MATTHEW 26:39

Do not be conformed to this world
but be transformed by the renewal of your mind,
that you may prove
what is the will of God,
what is good and acceptable and perfect.

ROMANS 12:2

Therefore do not be foolish,
but understand
what the will of the Lord is.

EPHESIANS 5:17

Therefore, my beloved,
as you have always obeyed, so now,
not only as in my presence
but much more in my absence,
work out your own salvation with fear and trembling;
for God is at work in you,
both to will and to work for his good pleasure.

PHILIPPIANS 2:12–13

Rejoice always, pray constantly,
give thanks in all circumstances;
for this is the will of God
in Christ Jesus
for you.

I THESSALONIANS 5:16–18

Instead you ought to say,
"If the Lord wills,
we shall live
and we shall do this or that."

JAMES 4:15

And this is the confidence
which we have in him,
that if we ask anything
according to his will
he hears us.

I JOHN 5:14

Thy kingdom come, Thy will be done,
On earth as it is in heaven.

MATTHEW 6:10

Let not your hearts be troubled;
believe in God,
believe also in me.

JOHN 14:1

Trust in the Lord
with all your heart,
and do not rely
on your own insight.

PROVERBS 3:5

We know that in everything
God works for good
with those who love him,
who are called
according to his purpose.

ROMANS 8:28

Prayer

Heavenly Father, we give thanks for the opportunity to communicate with You through the reading of the scriptures and prayer. We praise You for the Christian guidance that we receive from those who are called to Your purpose. We acknowledge that there are times when we want to stay still, and You require us to move. We acknowledge that there are times when we want to move, and You require us to stay still. We ask that our hearts and minds would be open as You communicate Your will to us. Please help us to maintain the focus and self-discipline necessary to follow Your will once we understand it. Help us to keep our trust in You in all matters as we seek to grow in faith and to forgive others as You have forgiven us.

NINE

Lord, Help Me Hold My Tongue

Some say that the world is made up of givers and takers. I experience it to be made up of encouragers and squashers. Some people use their words to make others feel better about themselves, to give hope in troubled times, or to impart wisdom for solving problems. Other people use their words to insult, inflame, or demean. Sometimes telling off a neighbor or loved one is just an outlet for handling frustration, but there is damage done in the process. Both adults and children can be uplifted or devastated by others' words.

A friend had slipped on wet pavement following a casual lunch and injured her spine. She was treated in the emergency room and was scheduled for surgery a few days later. As she went under the anesthesia, she began praying aloud that God would help guide the surgeon's hands to bring relief and healing. After surgery the surgeon came to see her and graciously stated, "Thank you for praying for me. I need all the help I can get." He continued, "I want to show you what went into your back to separate the two discs." He pulled something out of his pocket that looked like hardened putty in the shape of a cross. My friend smiled and thanked him for the job he had done. The pain relief was instant, and she was again able to move about without help. She also thanked God for answering her prayer.

The words spoken both by the patient and by the surgeon were encouraging and uplifting in a difficult and uncertain time. A mutual faith was shared between two believers as God was openly included in the procedure. That faith was shared with others in the operating room as well.

In contrast, I recall hearing a customer verbally annihilate a sales clerk in a nearby mall. The sales clerk stood motionless without a change of facial expression and allowed the customer to finish. At the end of the woman's verbal tirade, the clerk quietly and calmly responded, "I forgive you for your hurtful comments." It may be difficult to understand how the clerk could have remained so calm under attack, but we are given biblical instruction in Ephesians 6 on how to remain strong at such times without being doormats. We are to put on the armor of God in order to be protected from the hurt that others attempt to inflict. We are to gird our loins with the truth, put on the breastplate of righteousness, and shod our feet with the equipment of the gospel of peace. We are to take the shield of faith, with which we can quench the flaming darts of the evil one, to take the helmet of salvation, and the sword of the Spirit, which is the word of God. We are to pray at all times in the Spirit and to keep alert with perseverance.

More amazing than the response of the sales clerk was the response of the angry customer when she did not get back what she was dishing out. She appeared to acknowledge her inappropriateness and became embarrassed. No one consoled her. Her darts had circled back and were hitting her instead of the target. The pain she was trying to inflict on another was inflicted only on herself.

A short time later I was preparing for a parent-teacher conference. Previous teachers had warned me of that particular parent's vicious nature, and I prepared myself spiritually by reading the scripture several times about wearing God's armor for protection. As a result, I found myself sitting calmly for forty minutes while the parent told me every fault she perceived me to have. None of her words pierced my heart. I just felt sad for her outlook and sorry for her child. Normally I would sit during such a conference and think to myself, "God just sent this person into my life to entertain me." Then I would bite my tongue to keep from saying, "Thank you very much. I hope if I ever do anything right, you will feel free to share that with me, too." However, in my new suit of armor I did not have to become defensive or use humorous distraction as a means of survival. The fight was being fought on my behalf, and the child's welfare remained the only concern.

When the parent finished I was able to calmly respond, "You are absolutely right. I have been highly deficient in meeting this student's needs. What are some ways we can work together to help your child?" She was totally taken back and, ironically, was left speechless. It had probably never occurred to her that there might be some solutions available that could be addressed after the yearly chewing-up-and-spitting-out ritual. As for me, I found great peace and productivity in being able to rise above personal emotions and concentrate on the child rather than the adult.

There are times when people need to hear the truth about themselves, but even truth is not within biblical instruction when spewed like venom. Delivery of the truth does not have to cripple the listener. When you flatten another person's ego, you often render that person useless to you, and they may eventually cut you off. Our words must be chosen carefully if we are to genuinely love our neighbor as we love ourselves.

Verbal delivery is addressed in a number of scriptures. We are told that love is not rude (I Corinthians 13:5), that what comes out of a man's mouth is what makes him unclean (Matthew 15:11), that a man's religion is vain without a tight reign on the tongue (James 1:26), and that the tongue is a fire that stains the whole body (James 3:6). We are reminded that a kind word makes a man glad (Proverbs 12:25) and that pleasant words promote persuasiveness (Proverbs 16:21), giving sweetness to the soul and health to the body (Proverbs 16:24). The words we use are particularly important when dealing with children. As a teacher I learned early on about the criticism trap. New teachers often seek to control the class by constantly criticizing children with the expectation that it will create change. However, in this busy society in which children usually spend more time with their teachers than their parents, children will often act out in order to get the attention they need or desire. That is, to a child hungry for attention, it can be more rewarding to have negative attention than to have no attention at all. Consequently, the more teachers criticize children for what they are doing wrong, the more the children continue that same behavior, and the more the teacher has to criticize them for the same things. The instructor becomes trapped in a habit of criticism, and the child becomes trapped in unproductive behavior. Negativity permeates the air, and self-esteem can become lowered for both the adult and the child.

It is just as easy to catch a child being good instead of being bad. There are creative techniques that adults can use to teach children how to develop intrinsic motivation for doing what is right. These techniques sometimes involve pairing praise with extrinsic rewards until praise in itself is enough. Eventually the child's own self-talk will replace the adult's praise. Behavior modification is no substitute for Christian parenting or instruction, but it can be a positive alternative to the criticism trap.

Unfortunately, children who grow up around excessive criticism learn to be critical adults. Psychologists tell us that we criticize others the most for that which we are guiltiest. It is called projection. You project your faults on others but do not necessarily see them in yourself. The Bible refers to this as seeing the speck in someone else's eye but not seeing the log in our own (Matthew 7:3).

Some people are equally critical of themselves as they are

of others and suffer from even lower self-esteem through their own self-talk. Unkind words given to ourselves are just as detrimental as unkind words from others. Sometimes they are more detrimental because they are heard more frequently. If someone is repeatedly told he is worthless, he will become so. If an adult is repeatedly told she is ugly, she will respond as such. If you frequently tell yourself that you cannot be successful, you will not be. These are examples of self-fulfilling prophecies. Our thoughts inspire our actions and our responses. Scriptures advise us that the mouth speaks out of the overflow of the heart (Matthew 12:34). Genesis tells us that the world was spoken into existence by God. His words became a reality. We are made in His image. Our words can also create realities. Those realities can be created both in ourselves and in those over whom we have influence.

Forgiveness plays an integral part in our ability to overcome criticism. We have to forgive others continually for their insults or hurtful comments and move beyond them. We are called to let our neighbor know if we have been offended, but we are expected to do that without lowering ourselves to a level of destruction.

Forgiveness of self is also an integral part of our ability to overcome criticism. We have to pray for the ability to control the words we say both to others and to ourselves. Asking forgiveness does not guarantee that you will never say the wrong thing again. It means you have an awareness of the offense and a willingness to improve. Prayers to acquire more self-discipline are answered when the desire to change is genuinely present.

God knows that our spirits are damaged in the process of failed human interaction. God loves us whether we are capable at the moment of forgiving others for their failures or not. However, He cannot pour His blessings upon us without forgiveness. Galatians 5:22-23 addresses the fruit of the spirit that God wants to pour upon us: love, joy, peace, patience, kindness, goodness, faithfulness, gentleness, and self-control. If we are too filled with the negative emotions attached to unforgiveness, we may not be able to receive those gifts. Sometimes we have to do what our minds tell us to do because scriptures require it, and then our hearts will catch up as healing comes and wholeness returns. It is a process that takes effort, and free will gives us the option of saying yes to making the effort and thriving or of saying no to the work involved and remaining stuck. The latter simply delays us along our spiritual journey. Sooner or later, we will comprehend that God loves us enough to discipline us regarding our failure to forgive ourselves or others so that we can get back on track.

We cannot control the path that others take in terms of being an encourager or a squasher, but we can control our own. Reading scriptures about the tongue on a regular basis and praying about the quality of our verbal interaction with others is a beginning.

If any one thinks he is religious,
and does not bridle his tongue
but deceives his heart,
this man's religion is vain.

JAMES 1:26

And the tongue is a fire.
The tongue is an unrighteous world
among our members,
staining the whole body,
setting on fire
the cycle of nature,
and set on fire by hell.

JAMES 3:6

Anxiety in a man's heart
weighs him down,
but a good word makes him glad.

PROVERBS 12:25

A word fitly spoken
is like apples of gold in a setting of silver.

PROVERBS 25:11

The wise of heart
is called a man of discernment,
and pleasant speech
increases persuasiveness.

PROVERBS 16:21

Pleasant words are like a honeycomb,
sweetness to the soul and health to the body.

PROVERBS 16:24

You brood of vipers!
How can you speak good, when you are evil?
For out of the abundance of the heart the mouth speaks.

MATTHEW 12:34

Not what goes into the mouth defiles a man,
but what comes out of the mouth,
this defiles a man.

MATTHEW 15:11

Love is patient and kind;
love is not jealous or boastful;
it is not arrogant or rude.
Love does not insist on its own way;
it is not irritable or resentful;
it does not rejoice at wrong, but rejoices in the right.
Love bears all things,
believes all things, hopes all things, endures all things.

I CORINTHIANS 13:4–7

But the fruit of the Spirit is love, joy, peace, patience,
kindness, goodness, faithfulness, gentleness, self-control;
against such there is no law.

GALATIANS 5:22–23

For if you forgive men their trespasses,
your heavenly Father also
will forgive you;
but if you do not forgive men
their trespasses,
neither will your Father forgive your trespasses.

MATTHEW 6:14–15

*Why do you see the speck that is in your brother's eye,
but do not notice the log that is in your own eye?*

MATTHEW 7:3

Finally, be strong in the Lord and in the strength of his might. Put on the whole armor of God, that you may be able to stand against the wiles of the devil. For we are not contending against flesh and blood, but against the principalities, against the powers, against the world rulers of this present darkness, against the spiritual hosts of wickedness in the heavenly places.

Therefore take the whole armor of God, that you may be able to withstand in the evil day, and having done all, to stand. Stand therefore, having girded your loins with truth, and having put on the breastplate of righteousness, and having shod your feet with the equipment of the gospel of peace; besides all these, taking the shield of faith, with which you can quench all the flaming darts of the evil one. And take the helmet of salvation, and the sword of the Spirit, which is the word of God.

Pray at all times in the Spirit, with all prayer and supplication. To that end keep alert with all perseverance, making supplication for all the saints, and also for me, that utterance may be given me in opening my mouth boldly to proclaim the mystery of the gospel, for which I am an ambassador in chains; that I may declare it boldly, as I ought to speak.

EPHESIANS 6:10–20

Prayer

Heavenly Father, we give thanks for the gift of verbal communication. We ask for wisdom and self-discipline as we use our words so that they might further Your kingdom. Keep us reminded that, by wearing Your armor, we are able to protect ourselves from the verbal tirades of those whose words can crush us. Help us to see our shortcomings that we might work to overcome them. Remind us to examine our criticism of others in order to determine if their faults are our own. Make us receptive to the words You provide for us that bring healing and spiritual growth, rather than condemnation. We ask that You would strengthen our faith and help us to be more forgiving, as we realize that it is only through Your loving grace and mercy that we are worthy.

Conclusion

A friend once shared, "I refuse to go to church. The people there are all just a bunch of hypocrites." The only truthful, logical, and loving response was to tell her that we ARE all sinners, both inside of the church and outside of it. A minister once stated that the church is not a museum of saints; it is a hospital for sinners. We DO all need God's forgiveness for our sins. We DO all need to forgive ourselves and others for sins. The alternative is that we live with unnecessary inner turmoil.

My friend then exclaimed, "I can't forgive what so-and-so did to me! It will take me years to get over it! It will be a long, long time before I get to a point where I can forgive that person for what has happened." Therein lies a misconception about forgiveness. Forgiveness is not an emotion. It is not something you feel. Forgiveness is an action. It is something that you do. Forgiveness is not something you do after you heal. It is a prescription for allowing the healing, for setting yourself free of the hurt. Sometimes we have to pray for God to forgive someone even when we don't feel like the asking is sincere or that forgiveness of the other party is warranted. However, if you pray that God will allow you to forgive the person who hurt you because your mind tells you it is the biblical response, then over time your heart will catch up to your mind. Wholeness will be the result.

Forgiveness is not just something you do for the other person. It is something you do for yourself. Forgiveness does not have to be a mutual acknowledgment that one person was right and one was wrong. It is a gift you give yourself so that the wound does not fester and infect other parts of the body or contaminate the lives of others. It is not necessary for the person or people who hurt you to ask for your forgiveness in order for you to give it. It is not even necessary for them to know you have forgiven them unless, of course, they seek their own inner peace in the asking and the knowing.

Forgiveness does not have to involve forgetting. Remembering can be a helpful tool that keeps us from repeating the same mistakes or putting ourselves in harm's way in the future. Forgiving is an action that we must practice, however, in order to keep our inner joy. It is a means that God has given us for taking control out of the hands of the person or people who hurt us so that they cannot continue to hurt us and subsequently keep us from His purposes. Through prayer we put the control and hurt in God's hands. He then gives control back to us through the inner joy that comes with healing. We learn that the only way to have power is to give power away. The forgiveness process can be both lengthy and painful. It is not necessarily the result of one quick prayer, and sometimes outside help is necessary in order to achieve forgiveness. Too many times people turn to self-medication or addictive behaviors in an attempt to block the pain. This only slows down the process. You cannot go around pain; you have to go through it.

It is through faith and forgiveness that God's blessings are poured down upon us and that our personal light continues to develop from a flicker to a beacon. It is through faith and forgiveness that we gain insight, inspiration, and the motivation to share our spiritual seasoning with others. As the layers of our own sins are peeled back by repentance and forgiveness, we are released from the discomfort of the burdens too heavy to carry alone. We are sustained through the reading of the scriptures, through the implementation of the principles revealed, through our interaction with other Christians, and through daily communication with God in prayer. The enlightenment that we receive in the process is what allows us to love God more deeply and others more effectively. All that we think, all that we say, and all that we do affects the will of the heart. May the tablets of your heart be engraved with all that is holy.

This is the message we have heard from him and proclaim to you, that God is light and in him is no darkness at all. If we say we have fellowship with him while we walk in darkness, we lie and do not live according to the truth; but if we walk in the light, as he is in the light, we have fellowship with one another, and the blood of Jesus his Son cleanses us from all sin.

If we say we have no sin, we deceive ourselves, and the truth is not in us.

If we confess our sins, he is faithful and just, and will forgive our sins and cleanse us from all unrighteousness.

I JOHN 1:5–9

Put on then,
as God's chosen ones,
holy and beloved, compassion, kindness,
lowliness, meekness, and patience,
forbearing one another and,
if one has a complaint against another,
forgiving each other;
as the Lord has forgiven you,
so you also must forgive.

COLOSSIANS 3:12–13

Now faith is the assurance
of things hoped for,
the conviction of things not seen.
For by it
the men of old received divine approval.

HEBREWS 11:1–2

Prayer

Heavenly Father, we love You. We love Your Son who died for our sins, and we love the Holy Spirit that dwells within us that allows Your light to shine through us.

We give thanks for the faith that prevails in our hearts and for Your promises that continue to go unchanged. We give thanks for the forgiveness that we are allowed to receive for our transgressions when we come forward as Christians with repentant hearts. We give thanks for the forgiveness that we are allowed to give to others, whether they ask for it or not, so that our own personal healing can ensue.

We ask that You would keep us reminded of our responsibility to share our inner light and spiritual seasoning with others. We ask that You would uplift us in times of trouble and remind us to seek out the lessons You desire for us to learn as we work through life's dilemmas. Help us to be released from our personal bondage and to become more useful to You through a growing faith and through a greater capacity to forgive. Keep us reminded that we can remain close to You through prayer, through Bible reading, and through worship and fellowship at church.

In Christ's name we pray,
Amen.

CPSIA information can be obtained
at www.ICGtesting.com
Printed in the USA
FSHW020148151220

9 781425 144012